CW00504229

"As chefs—and I am no exception—we often hope to re-create the comfort food from our own countries. This can be a difficult task because it involves both compromise and creativity. This duality is embedded in every single one of Rie's marvelous recipes. Her book taught me new things about familiar ingredients, and reconnected me with the wonderful Japanese home cooking that I have always loved."

—**Nobu Matsuhisa**, chef and owner, Nobu Restaurant Group

"*Make It Japanese* is the literary equivalent of umami. You know how when you taste something with umami, you can't stop eating it? With *Make It Japanese*, you can't stop reading it and you can't stop cooking from it. These are recipes you'll revel in over and over."

—**Dorie Greenspan**, *New York Times* bestselling cookbook author

"Rie has written a book that is full of amazing homestyle Japanese food that I *love* and want to eat every day. She makes the dream a reality with recipes that are as easy to follow as they are delicious. From oyako don to nabe and pickles, she hits all the favorites. Plus, she's the coolest cucumber on the planet. Run, don't walk, to this book."

—**Roy Choi**, chef and restaurateur

"Rie McClenny has packed a lot into *Make It Japanese*'s doable collection of recipes, straightforward pointers, and cultural tidbits. She has a knack for anticipating your questions and answers them succinctly. This is the book for anyone wanting unfussy, delicious Japanese home cooking."

—**Andrea Nguyen**, James Beard Award winner and author of *Ever-Green Vietnamese*

"Rie takes you on an amazing culinary journey of delicious Japanese recipes you can easily make at home with readily obtainable ingredients."

—**John Kanell**, *New York Times* bestselling author and founder of *Preppy Kitchen*

make it japanese

make it japanese

simple recipes for everyone

Rie McClenny

with Sanaë Lemoine

Photographs by Jeni Afuso

Clarkson Potter/Publishers
New York

For my mother, Yoko,
my husband, Blair,
and my son, Hugo

contents

introduction

If I told my seventeen-year-old self that I would be writing a cookbook, developing recipes, and making YouTube videos for a living, she would be very surprised. I think she would say: "Wait, why are you not a flight attendant?!"

And yet here I am, writing a book that reflects my journey as a Japanese woman living abroad for many years. No matter where I was during those years, whether West Virginia or New York, Orlando or Los Angeles, I sought to re-create the flavors of my Japanese upbringing using the ingredients I had available to me—first as a cure for my own homesickness, and now as part of raising my son, nourishing him with the foods my own mother cooked for me.

This book is proof that the tastes from home can be yours, no matter where you are. And for me, home began in Hiroshima, where the threads of inspiration for these Japanese recipes originated, then twisted and turned as I moved away and found my own culinary path, "making it Japanese"

wherever I went, and now stretching out to your home with this book.

I come from a small seaside city in the Hiroshima prefecture, in the southwestern part of Japan. My parents' house is surrounded by agricultural land, with the mountains on one side and the Seto Inland Sea on the other. We lived next door to my paternal grandfather, a retired police officer who grew tomatoes, cucumbers, sweet potatoes, and other vegetables in our shared garden. Every day, I rode my bicycle to school along the coast, breathing in the strong scent of oyster farms. We had access to an abundance of fresh seafood, and on weekends we would go clam digging.

My maternal grandmother ran a kissaten (Japanese tearoom and café) with my mom's help. She served simple, comforting meals, such as yakisoba in a sizzling cast-iron pan, fried rice, coffee jelly, and shaved ice in the summer. I spent much of my childhood at the kissaten, pouring water for

customers and chitchatting with them. Because my mom was a talented cook, I didn't feel the need to learn. Instead, I watched her for hours on end as she folded gyoza faster than my eyes could follow and never measured ingredients—one circular pour of soy sauce, a handful of bonito flakes, a dash of sake. In my spare time, I read cookbooks and food magazines and daydreamed of flavor combinations.

I also dreamed of living abroad. We didn't travel outside the country as a family, so my only exposure to English was a conversation class I took after school. I'm the eldest of three children, and my dad didn't want me to move far away, but I was determined to study abroad. Encouraged by my mom, I found several opportunities to travel: first a homestay of two weeks in Brisbane, Australia, followed by a month-long exchange program in Melbourne.

However, according to my uncle, the best way to see the world was as a flight attendant. He suggested I study at a junior college where many of the graduates go on to become flight attendants. I embarked on this path, although deep down I knew it was an excuse to leave Japan and not my true passion. I didn't get any of the flight attendant jobs, and eventually I transferred to a four-year college where I majored in English.

My first time traveling to the United States was for a year-abroad program through my university in Osaka. They chose a city in West Virginia, which seemed close to New York on a map. Imagine my surprise when I arrived! In some ways, the rural area reminded me of my hometown, although I missed being by the sea. I lived in a house with several other exchange students. Being away from Japan for such a long stretch made me more aware of my heritage.

There was only one Asian supermarket close by—a tiny grocery store with a mishmash of ingredients from all over Asia—but I found sake, mirin, and soy sauce. I realized that with those three ingredients, and if I was creative in adapting my mom's recipes, I could appease my homesickness.

After college, I moved to Orlando for thirteen months to work at Disney World's Japan Pavilion. There were about thirty of us, all women aged twenty to thirty-five. We formed a tight-knit group. Like during my year abroad in West Virginia, we cooked to satiate our childhood cravings, but we had to compromise with the ingredients we found at the local grocery stores, often searching for substitutes to conjure those flavors we so missed.

By then, I think my parents realized I might never permanently move back to Japan, though I did return for a few years. I worked for a company in Tokyo that helped exchange students. One of our clients was a Japanese culinary school, and they asked me to organize a tour of culinary schools in New York. Within a few months, I was hired to be the school's translator and event coordinator.

We invited famous French chefs for demos, and I would translate from English to Japanese. (Most of the chefs spoke very good English.) I loved how passionate and demanding the students were, often coming in on weekends or when the school was closed. As I listened to the chefs, I absorbed their knowledge without quite understanding what they were saying. It was like translating someone's words without grasping their exact meaning. I was drawn to this world and yet afraid to dive in. I knew culinary school was expensive, and I wasn't sure I could shoulder the pressure.

In 2007, the culinary school asked me to open their pâtisserie café in New York. During that time, I met my husband and decided to make the US my home. So began my real immersion in food, first at the café, then at a Japanese restaurant in Midtown specializing in sake, and finally at Korin, a Japanese knife and kitchenware store in Tribeca. Although I enjoyed my work, something wasn't quite right. I was surrounded by ambitious people who were following their dreams, but what about my own ambitions? For years, I had been thinking about culinary

school without taking the plunge. I decided it was time—after all, I had enough savings and had found a program that allowed me to continue working full time at Korin. So, at the age of thirty-three, I finally enrolled at the French Culinary Institute.

When I wasn't in class, I perused issues of *Gourmet* and dreamed of becoming a food stylist, but first I wanted to gain real kitchen experience. After culinary school, I moved to Los Angeles with my husband and worked in the kitchens of Jeremy Fox at Rustic Canyon and Suzanne Goin at AOC. These two chefs had a profound impact on my cooking: They stretched my skills and taught me to see ingredients in entirely new ways. Thanks to them, I started to incorporate French techniques in my Japanese cooking and used local, seasonal produce from the farmers' market.

One day, after an especially grueling shift of working more than three hundred covers, I came across a job posting at BuzzFeed for a recipe developer who spoke Japanese, had a culinary degree and professional kitchen experience, and lived in LA. The position seemed too good to be true. I applied, and a few weeks later, I started working at Tasty Japan, the Japanese edition of BuzzFeed's food media brand, Tasty, while continuing my restaurant job. In the mornings, I developed recipes, and from 3:30 p.m. to midnight, I cooked at AOC. Despite the long days, it was exhilarating to finally pursue what I loved.

When I first moved to the US, I didn't have many friends and I was nervous going to dinner parties because I wasn't completely comfortable speaking in English. I was afraid of not knowing what to talk about with strangers. Food became a survival skill, a way to find common ground. As an icebreaker, I would ask: "What is your favorite restaurant?" I liked how animated people became when describing food they loved. One woman told me about a French pastry shop that also made Armenian pastries on the side. She ordered me to not get any of the French pastries and instead try the Armenian

cream-filled doughnuts called ponchiks. Her descriptions were so detailed and her enthusiasm so palpable that I had to find out for myself! Another person told me about the birthday cake his mom would make for him, and how the floor of her kitchen was slanted so the cake always came out of the oven uneven with one side more raised than the other. His mother would even out the cake with frosting, and he'd always eat a slice from the "lower" side as it had a thicker layer of frosting. Everyone had strong opinions and stories about food, and I never tired of hearing them.

I got into the habit of bringing Japanese home-style dishes to dinner parties, and inevitably we would talk about the food. Maybe someone would ask about the ingredients, maybe they would discover something new about Japanese food. I soon realized that most people were not familiar with Japanese home cooking. There was an assumption that Japanese food was either a multicourse sushi extravaganza or a theatrical Benihana-style teppanyaki with onion volcanoes, when in reality Japanese home cooking is simple, humble, and nutritious. Meat is often an accompaniment rather than the main ingredient, while vegetables take center stage. We like to use fresh ingredients and favor quick, unfussy preparations.

When cooking for my American friends, I wanted to showcase the simple beauty of Japanese cuisine—how, at its heart, it is about allowing ingredients to really shine. How the balance of flavors—salt from soy sauce, acidity from sake, sweetness from mirin—reveals an ingredient's true potential and flavor. For instance, kabocha squash simmered in a concentrated broth brings out the vegetable's natural sweetness. Most important, I wanted to show how Japanese home cooking can be for everyone.

In the fifteen years I've lived in America, I have sought to re-create the flavors of my family's recipes while using ingredients that are easy to find and sometimes substituting when the Japanese ingredient isn't readily available. Some recipes have stayed the same, such as the steamed cakes my mom made for an afternoon snack when I came home from school (see page 211). Others have been transformed: Miso soup is traditionally eaten as a light broth for breakfast or a side dish, but on cold winter evenings, I like to make a hearty version with kale and sweet potatoes (Loaded Vegetable Miso Soup, page 34). Or the sake-steamed clams (see page 110), to which I've added plenty of butter, a technique I learned from Suzanne Goin. Often the exercise of adapting these recipes has led me to delicious, unexpected outcomes, such as my roasted cauliflower with a toasted sesame dressing (see page 41).

This cookbook draws inspiration from the nourishing food my mom cooked throughout my childhood and my extensive knowledge of Japanese cuisine and ingredients that I've brought to life in an American kitchen. In making the Japanese dishes I love, many of which are typically bought premade in Japan or ones that I simply let my mom cook for me in the past, I've learned to prepare them from scratch, often using only ingredients from my local

supermarket. What seemed like a compromise when I first came to the US as an exchange student no longer feels that way today. If anything, it can be a wonderful discovery, like learning about Salted Rhubarb Paste (page 58) to replace umeboshi (pickled plum; see page 22) or making my own curry roux instead of using the boxed cubes (see Curry Rice, page 73).

In this book, I will teach you the building blocks of Japanese home cooking and how to stock a Japanese pantry using mostly ingredients you can find at your neighborhood grocery store. I'll offer alternatives for specialty items, show you easy Japanese cooking techniques, and introduce you to flavor combinations that I hope you'll savor as much as I do.

I've divided the book into chapters that illustrate the way we eat at home in Japan. Some dishes are small and meant to be served with other dishes to form a complete meal, while others are filling one-bowl recipes that will satisfy you on your hungriest days. Many of these recipes come together quickly on a busy weeknight, whereas others require a bit more preparation for when you want to gather around a feast with friends and family. I hope this book can be your entryway into Japanese home cooking, and that soon you'll find yourself applying these flavors and techniques to your favorite ingredients.

When I shoot a video, I always think about the person cooking on the other side: How can I make this recipe easier and more accessible? How can I make it less intimidating? Japanese home cooking isn't meant to be precious or overly complicated. Regardless of your abilities—whether you're a beginner or a seasoned cook—you really can prepare all of the dishes in this book. Don't be afraid to make mistakes because you will, and I promise I do, too. At the end of the day, cooking is about nourishment and enjoying the act of making a meal for yourself and others. I hope that you find such joy and inspiration in these pages.

how to stock a japanese pantry

調味料の選び方

Every cuisine has its signature seasoning. In Japanese cooking, the main ingredients for imparting flavor are miso, soy sauce, mirin, sake, and dashi. If you have these five ingredients, you can cook almost every savory recipe in this book. Most of these items are shelf-stable, so they'll last a long time. There are also a handful of other Japanese ingredients, which I will cover in this section, that are delicious and worth seeking out for the recipes in this book. In this section, I've listed some of the brands I used for this book, especially for ingredients where I think it matters most to select a specific variety or brand. Japanese grocery stores will offer many options for each ingredient, and even for me, the abundance of choices can at times be a bit overwhelming. I prefer Japanese brands or ingredients made in Japan, as their flavors are closest to the food I ate growing up. I've also found that a higher price for a Japanese ingredient usually indicates better quality.

Most of the components for a Japanese pantry can be found at your neighborhood grocery store, health and natural foods stores, or online. However, if you can, I also recommend trekking to a Japanese or Asian grocery store since the ingredients tend to be more reasonably priced, you can get bigger bags of rice, and you'll have more variety to choose from. Don't forget to pick up some Japanese snacks on your way out! I've included my favorites on page 20.

Sake 酒

Sake is a Japanese rice wine with 13% to 17% alcohol content. If you go to a Japanese or Asian grocery store, you may find sake bottles that are labeled "cooking sake (料理酒)" in the pantry section. This "cooking sake" contains additives, including salt, and isn't drinkable. My mom once gave me the advice to choose a sake that tastes good enough to drink, so I use regular sake in the kitchen. You can find sake at liquor stores, and sometimes even at American grocery stores. I like to cook with junmai (a type of sake that is brewed with pure rice) and recommend the brand Shochikubai for an affordable and easy-to-find option. (The bottles should be around $10.) Make sure you don't buy nigori, a cloudy sake that tends to be sweeter and isn't suitable for cooking. If you cannot find regular sake, and if "cooking sake" is the only available option, you can use it, but the flavor of the dish will be quite different, and personally I much prefer the flavor imparted by regular sake.

Mirin みりん

Mirin is a sweet rice wine with an alcohol content of 8% to 14%. There are several varieties of mirin. I usually choose hon mirin, which translates to "real" or "true" mirin. There are "impostor" types of mirin that you will want to avoid, as they contain a lot of additives, such as corn syrup. These are usually labeled "mirin type" or "aji-mirin." Take a look at the ingredient list and check whether the first ingredient is corn syrup or glucose syrup. Ideally, choose a mirin that has as the first ingredient rice or sake. Those will have a natural and delicate sweetness.

Soy Sauce 醤油

Soy sauce is made from fermenting soybeans and has a salty, deep, rich flavor. Japan's neighboring countries all make soy sauce, but the methods and ingredients are different. All the recipes in this book were developed with Japanese soy sauce, called shoyu. The most widely known and accessible brand in the US is Kikkoman. I like their organic soy sauce (regular). For a gluten-free option, you can use tamari, knowing that tamari is richer in flavor and a bit thicker in texture, so you may have to use less than the recipe amount. Taste and adjust the amount as desired. The same applies for reduced-sodium soy sauce—just make sure to taste the dish as you season and add more or less depending on your preference.

Cooking Alphabet 料理のさしすせそ

There is a Japanese cooking acronym that goes like this: "Sa (sugar) Shi (salt) Su (vinegar) Se (soy sauce) So (miso)." It dictates the order in which you add ingredients to a braised dish (nimono). First sugar, then salt, followed by vinegar, and finally soy sauce and miso. I've known "sa shi su se so" for as long as I can remember, though I assumed it was an old wives' tale. But when I looked into the meaning behind it, I realized that it's actually based on science. Since the molecule for sugar (satō in Japanese) is bigger than salt (shio in Japanese), you want to add sugar before salt. This way, the ingredient can better absorb the sugar first and then the salt. If you add vinegar too early in the cooking process, its sharpness is lost. Soy sauce and miso are both fermented foods, so you'll want to add them in the final stages of cooking to maintain their flavor and aroma. Of course, not all recipes follow this exact order when incorporating ingredients, but I've found it helpful as a general guideline.

Miso 味噌

Miso is a fermented soybean paste made from soybeans, salt, and koji. (Koji is a type of mold culture.) It contains probiotics and has many health benefits. Here in the US, miso is mainly categorized by color—yellow, red, and white—but there are many other varieties and each region in Japan has its own miso. My friend Ai, the owner of the artisanal miso company Omiso, likens miso to wine: "Different regions make different types of miso that suit their climate." Store it in the refrigerator and make sure to always use clean utensils when scooping it out. Of the common categorizations of miso in the US, red tends to be saltier and white is the sweetest and mildest of the three, whereas yellow is somewhere in the middle. It's difficult to recommend one type of miso, as each one has a slightly different flavor, and the best way to find your favorite is to taste and see what you like. You can use any miso paste for the recipes in this book—just make sure to taste as you cook and adjust the amount to your preference. If you have never cooked with miso before and are looking for a specific recommendation, I like Hikari Miso's koji miso, which is available at Japanese grocery stores, and amakuchi yellow miso from Omiso (they ship nationwide). For an American brand, I often use the light yellow miso from Cold Mountain.

Sugar 砂糖

As you cook from this book, you may be surprised by how often I use sugar in my savory recipes. It's an important ingredient in Japanese cooking: It rounds out the sharpness of rice vinegar and highlights the natural sweetness of other ingredients. In contrast, Japanese desserts are usually less sweet than Western desserts. A friend once told me that one of the reasons we include a bit of sugar in our savory dishes is so that our brain and palate are satisfied with the sweetness. It makes us less likely to crave a sweet dessert right after the meal. The sugar we use for cooking in Japan is a little different from the cane sugar in the US: The grains are finer, and it has a higher moisture content, making it dissolve more readily. For my recipes, I used regular American granulated sugar.

Rice Vinegar 米酢

Rice vinegar has a milder flavor and cleaner aftertaste than distilled white vinegar. Its color is pale amber and it is essential for making sushi rice and sunomono (pickled salad). Avoid "sushi vinegar," which is already seasoned and tends to be too sweet. My favorite brands for rice vinegar are Mizkan and Marukan.

Rice 米

Most of the dishes in this book are meant to be served with a bowl of white rice. I recommend using short-grain rice, or medium-grain rice as an alternative. I usually buy the Koshihikari (こしひかり) brand, which you can find at Japanese grocery stores. See more about rice on page 115.

Nori 海苔

Nori are thin sheets of roasted seaweed. We often use nori to wrap rice, either as an onigiri (rice ball), hand roll, or from a bowl of rice. (If you are eating nori with rice from a bowl, place a small piece of nori over some rice and use your chopsticks to wrap the nori around the rice.) I like to use seasoned nori (ajitsuke nori) for onigiri and unseasoned nori for sushi. Once you open a package, store it in a resealable plastic bag in a dry, cool, and dark place for up to 1 month. The nori will lose its crispiness over time. When this happens, lightly toast it on both sides in a skillet until crisp.

Kombu 昆布

Kombu, or dried kelp, is an essential ingredient for making dashi (see page 31) and sauces, such as the sweet soy sauce in my mazemen recipes. It adds a subtle but important layer of umami. Use kitchen shears or scissors to cut the kombu into the desired size. If you go to a Japanese grocery store and see many varieties, I recommend rausu kombu (羅臼昆布) for making vegan kombu dashi, as it'll impart a more intense kombu flavor. If you are making awase dashi with katsuobushi (bonito flakes), I recommend using rishiri kombu (利尻昆布) or ma kombu (真昆布), which are my preferred kinds for blending with katsuobushi. You can also find kombu at most American grocery stores, where it is usually simply labeled as "kelp" or "kombu." (Look for the Eden and Emerald Cove brands.) Kombu is sensitive to humidity, so once you open the package, store it in a resealable plastic bag or an airtight container in a dry, cool, and dark place for up to 1 year.

Bonito Flakes 鰹節

Known as katsuobushi in Japanese, bonito flakes are shavings of dried, aged bonito fish. They are used to make a rich umami-flavored dashi, and as a topping for savory food. When the flakes are placed on hot food, such as okonomiyaki (cabbage pancakes), they move with the residual heat, as though they are "dancing." Katsuobushi has a very distinct woody and smoky scent—one friend aptly described it as opening an old wooden cabinet that has been closed for a while. The flavor isn't salty but reminds me a bit of smoked fish. It's easy to find in American grocery stores (look for the Eden brand). If you go to a Japanese grocery store, you can find more options, in which case I recommend choosing one that is portioned in individual small bags. This way, the katsuobushi will stay fresh for longer. Once you open the package, store it in a resealable plastic bag and freeze for up to 6 months.

Dashi Powder だしの素

Dashi powder, or instant dashi, is a convenient alternative to homemade dashi, especially when you only need a small amount. Make sure to adjust the seasoning, as some dashi powders contain

salt. There are many brands, though the one that's easiest to find in the US is by Ajinomoto and comes in different flavors, such as hondashi (with bonito) and kombu dashi (with kelp, for a vegan option).

Dashi Pack だしパック

Dashi packs are another great alternative for making dashi from scratch. Unlike dashi powder, the whole ingredients—such as shaved bonito, dried anchovies, and kombu—are blended and portioned into small tea bag–like bags. You soak the pack in hot water to make the dashi. You can find these online or at Japanese grocery stores.

Neutral Oil サラダ油

For this book, I mainly used grapeseed oil, which is my preferred neutral oil. But you can use canola or any other vegetable oil of your choice.

Toasted Sesame Oil ごま油

Toasted sesame oil is very fragrant and has a lovely nutty flavor. I use it to season my dishes and rarely call on it for my main "cooking" oil. I like the Kadoya brand, which you can easily find at American or Japanese and Asian grocery stores. I recommend storing it in the refrigerator.

Panko パン粉

Panko are Japanese bread crumbs. They're bigger and lighter than Italian bread crumbs, so they provide a nice crunchy texture, especially for fried foods like tonkatsu (pork cutlets). They're widely available at American grocery stores.

Mochiko もち粉

Mochiko is a type of glutinous sweet rice flour with a fine powdery texture. Once baked or cooked, it lends that signature chewy texture you find in mochi, a Japanese rice cake. It's increasingly

My Favorite
Japanese Grocery
Store Snacks

If you're ever at a Japanese grocery store
replenishing your pantry, make sure to take
home a few sweet and savory snacks, as they are
very different from American snacks. The flavors
and textures will surprise you.
Here are my favorites:

GALBO
Chocolate cookies enveloped in dark chocolate.
This has been my favorite chocolate snack since
I was a teenager.

JAGARIKO
Super-crunchy potato sticks.

IKATEN SETOUCHI LEMON
Sour and salty fried squid, made in Hiroshima!

FUWATTO MEIJIN
Airy rice puffs that make you feel
like you're eating clouds.

CALBEE POTATO CHIPS
These are thinner than American chips and
coated with a perfect amount of seasoning
(for someone who thinks American chips
are overseasoned!). My favorite flavors are
consommé, soy sauce, and hot and spicy.

available at American grocery stores. I like to use Koda Farms mochiko, which is available online. Make sure to buy mochiko and not rice flour, which is completely different in texture and flavor, and cannot be used as a substitute.

Shiratamako 白玉粉

Shiratamako is another type of glutinous sweet rice flour. It's processed differently from mochiko and has an entirely different texture. It almost looks like dried feta and is a bit chalky. This flour is harder to find in the US, but I prefer it for making dango (see Dango Miso Soup, page 37) and mochi as it yields a much silkier and chewier texture. You can find it at Japanese grocery stores or online. If you can't find shiratamako, substitute with mochiko.

Aburaage 油揚げ

A deep-fried tofu pouch, aburaage tends to be oily when you use it straight from the package. To remove the excess oil, place the aburaage in a fine-mesh sieve or colander and pour hot water over the pouches. This process of removing the oil is called abura nuki (油抜き). You'll find aburaage in the tofu or frozen food section at Japanese or Asian grocery stores.

Kewpie Mayonnaise キユーピーマヨネーズ

This Japanese mayonnaise is richer and more flavorful than American brands of mayonnaise. It's a bit savory and has a touch of MSG or yeast extract, and it's a bit eggy, too, since it's made from just egg yolks and not the whole egg. I've seen it at many American supermarkets in the condiment aisle; otherwise, you'll easily find it at Japanese or Asian grocery stores.

Okonomiyaki Sauce お好み焼きソース

Okonomiyaki sauce almost tastes like barbecue sauce, but not quite. It's sweetened with dates and has spiced afternotes. I'm a huge fan of the Otafuku brand. You'll need it for drizzling on my Mini Okonomiyaki (cabbage pancakes; page 174), and you can also use it as a tonkatsu (pork cutlet) dipping sauce. You can purchase it online and at Japanese grocery stores.

Tonkatsu Sauce とんかつソース

A little runnier than okonomiyaki sauce, tonkatsu sauce is closer to Worcestershire sauce. It's salty, sweet, and a bit acidic. It soaks perfectly into the tonkatsu (pork cutlets) and is a must-have ingredient for the katsu sando (pork cutlet sandwich). I recommend the Bull-Dog brand, which is available online and at Japanese grocery stores. In a pinch, you can make a homemade version by combining 3 tablespoons Worcestershire sauce, 2 tablespoons ketchup, and 1 tablespoon honey.

Soba Noodles そば

Soba noodles are made with buckwheat. There are several kinds, but if you'd like a gluten-free variety, make sure to look for jūwari soba (十割そば), which is made with 100% buckwheat. Most other soba noodles are a blend of wheat and buckwheat flours. The most popular blend is nihachi soba (二八そば) and is made of 80% buckwheat and 20% wheat. It's easy to find at American, Japanese, and Asian grocery stores.

Ramen Noodles 中華麺

I tested all my ramen recipes with Sun Noodle's "kaedama noodles." Many famous ramen restaurants use Sun Noodle ramen. These noodles are becoming easier to find at American grocery stores, usually in the fresh or frozen section. Otherwise, you can find fresh ramen noodles at Japanese or Asian grocery stores. As an alternative, you can use my Spaghetti Baking Soda Hack (page 155).

Udon Noodles うどん

A thick noodle made with wheat flour, udon is available fresh, frozen, or dried at Japanese grocery stores. Fresh and frozen udon will be thick and chewy, whereas dried udon will be thinner with a different texture, but all work well for the recipes in this book. If you can easily find frozen or fresh udon noodles, I recommend using them. My favorite are Sanuki udon, which have a chewier, springy texture than other brands. (Sanuki is a region in Kagawa prefecture in Japan famous for its chewy udon noodles.)

Umeboshi 梅干し

Umeboshi is a salt-pickled plum. It is very sour, salty, and alkaline. In Japan, umeboshi is known for its health benefits, and whenever I was sick, my mom would make rice porridge with umeboshi. There are several kinds, but my favorite is umeboshi pickled with honey, as it's milder in flavor. I recommend trying that one first. I've been seeing umeboshi at health food stores and American supermarkets, like Whole Foods. Otherwise, you can easily find it at Japanese grocery stores, where you'll have plenty of varieties to choose from.

Shichimi Togarashi 七味唐辛子

Shichimi togarashi is a Japanese crushed red pepper blend made of a combination of seven ingredients, often including crushed red pepper (togarashi), sesame seeds, citrus peel, and other spices and ingredients. (Shichi means "seven" in Japanese.) It gives a nice spicy kick to udon noodle soups or hot pot dipping sauces. You can find it at any Japanese or Asian grocery store in the spice section.

Roasted Sesame Seeds 炒りごま

There are two kinds of roasted sesame seeds, white sesame (白ごま) and black sesame (黒ごま). White sesame seeds have a milder nutty flavor, whereas black sesame seeds have a slightly stronger flavor with a hint of bitterness. I mostly use white sesame seeds, though I'll use black sesame seeds when they are a central ingredient, like in a dessert. If you can't find roasted sesame seeds, you can toast them in a small dry skillet over medium heat. You can buy them in bigger quantities at Japanese or Asian grocery stores. For instructions on how to grind sesame seeds, see Roasted Cauliflower Goma-ae, page 41.

Matcha 抹茶

Matcha is a powder made from finely ground green tea leaves. Thanks to the recent matcha boom in the US, it's much easier to find at regular supermarkets and health food stores. There are two types of matcha: ceremonial grade and culinary grade. You can use the less expensive culinary grade for all my recipes, but for a very bright, vibrant green color, I recommend ceremonial-grade matcha.

Adzuki Beans 小豆

The main ingredient for making anko (Sweet Red Bean Paste, page 227) is adzuki. Once cooked, the small beans are creamy and a little sweet. You can find dried adzuki beans at Japanese and Asian grocery stores or at health food stores. Unlike other beans, you don't need to soak them overnight.

How to Make a Parchment Cartouche

In Japanese cooking, we often use a wooden drop-lid called an otoshibuta (落とし蓋). The lid is slightly smaller than the pot. It fits inside the pot and rests directly on the braising liquid. It traps the steam and reduces evaporation but is lightweight enough that it doesn't squash the ingredients. These lids are hard to find in the US, so I've started using a French cooking tool called a cartouche. It's a round of parchment paper that mimics the otoshibuta. Follow the instructions below for how to make a parchment cartouche:

1. Cut a square of parchment paper that's slightly bigger than your cooking vessel.

2. Fold one corner over to the opposite side to create a triangle shape, then fold again to create a smaller triangle shape.

3. Repeat the fold to create a smaller triangle shape. Fold over again to create a cone (like an ice cream cone).

4. Place the cone flat over the top of the cooking vessel, with the tip of the cone at the center of the vessel.

5. Using scissors, cut the "ice cream" end of the cone (the one opposite the tip) so it's the same length as the radius of the vessel.

6. Unfold the paper and use it as a lid. (You can also use this technique to make a round cake liner.)

essential japanese kitchen tools

There are a few Japanese kitchen tools that I cannot live without. You don't need all these tools to cook from my book, but they'll make it much easier, and you may even find yourself using them for your everyday cooking. You can find these tools online, at most Japanese grocery stores, and at Japanese tableware stores such as Korin, Toiro, and Mutual Trading Company (MTC).

Knives 包丁

At one time, I worked at Korin, a Japanese knife and tableware store in New York City. I learned so much about Japanese knives, specifically how they are lighter than Western knives because the blades tend to be thinner. As a result, they're generally more comfortable to use. It's important not to cut a very hard item like frozen food or an avocado pit. If you don't already have a set of knives you like, I recommend choosing these three knives: a chef's knife (mine is 8.2 inches), a petty knife (about

6 inches), and a bread knife. Petty knives are useful for cutting smaller items, such as garlic and fruits. My favorite knife brands are Misono and Nenox. Japanese knives should stay sharp for a long time and will last a lifetime. Make sure to treat them well and sharpen them whenever they start to feel blunt. Of course, feel free to use Western knives if you already own them and have a preferred kind.

Cooking Chopsticks 菜箸

Most Japanese home cooks use chopsticks as their primary cooking utensil. Cooking chopsticks are called saibashi in Japanese and are longer than the ones used for eating. They're one of my favorite tools, and once you've gotten the hang of them, you'll find that they're very versatile and easy to use. You can mix eggs the way you would with a fork, stir in a skillet instead of using a spatula, or use them as more precise tongs for picking up hot items. Since they're made of wood and quite light, be careful to keep them far away from the flame if you have a gas stove. You can find them online or at most Japanese grocery stores.

Mesh Skimmer あくとり

A mesh skimmer is called aku tori in Japanese. It's shaped like a ladle with a long handle and a fine-mesh sieve instead of a spoon. We use it for skimming impurities when braising or simmering. You'll see that several recipes in this book call for skimming impurities off the top of a broth as they rise to the surface during cooking, which results in a clearer broth. It's an essential part of Japanese cooking. In a pinch, you can use a spoon, but it'll be harder to catch the impurities without also getting the cooking liquid. Although a mesh skimmer isn't a "must-have" item, once you have it, you won't be able to live without it. (It's also a wonderful tool to use for removing small solids when shallow or deep-frying, especially between batches.)

Mandoline スライサー

I love using a mandoline to thinly slice big quantities of vegetables, like a head of cabbage, or when you need uniform slices, such as garlic chips or cucumber for sunomono (pickled salad). Just be careful when using this tool, as the blade is incredibly sharp, and it's easy to accidentally slice the tips of your fingers! I usually hold the ingredient with a kitchen towel to protect my fingers.

Thermometer 調理用温度計

I often use an instant-read food thermometer, especially when I'm deep-frying, to check the temperature of the oil. Some of my recipes call for different oil temperatures and require a thermometer. Once you're more comfortable in the kitchen, you'll know the temperature of the oil from visual and sound cues, but as a beginner, a thermometer is a great item to keep in your kitchen. You can also use it for checking the temperature of meat.

Tamagoyaki Pan 卵焼き器

A tamagoyaki pan is a special rectangular pan for making Tamagoyaki (rolled omelet, page 84). The traditional pans are made from copper, but if you're a beginner, I recommend using a nonstick pan as it'll be much easier to shape the omelet. You can also use a small round nonstick skillet; it'll be harder to make the iconic rectangular log shape, but once you cut off the ends you can hardly tell the difference. You can find tamagoyaki pans at most Japanese grocery stores and online.

Electric Rice Cooker 炊飯器

At home, I have two kinds of Japanese rice cookers: the 5.5-cup Zojirushi, one of the most common electric rice cookers, and the cast-iron Vermicular. I've included instructions for cooking rice on the stove (see page 118), but depending on how many people you have in your household, how busy your schedule is, and how much space you have in your kitchen, you might consider an electric rice cooker. They come in different sizes and there are many brands. The Vermicular, which can also be used as an induction burner for braises and stews, yields beautifully cooked rice, but it is very expensive. My personal favorite is the 5.5-cup Zojirushi. It's a wonderful, practical appliance: You just wash the rice, add water, and press the "on" button. Rice cookers also keep the rice hot for several hours, so you can set it before going to bed or in the morning before leaving for work, and the rice will be ready when you wake up or come home.

Cutting Board まな板

When using Japanese knives, I recommend a hinoki (Japanese cypress) cutting board. Hinoki is softer than plastic or other woods, such as bamboo, and helps keep your knife's blade sharp for longer. The cypress wood has a lovely scent, too, and is known to have natural antibacterial properties. You can sometimes find them at Japanese grocery stores or otherwise online.

Donabe 土鍋

A donabe is a Japanese clay pot. It's perfect for hot pots and rice, but you can also use it for many other dishes, such as Oyako Don (chicken and egg rice bowl, page 121), Soy Sauce–Simmered Kabocha (page 38), and Nikujaga (beef and potato stew, page 82). It's made of clay and is quite thick, so it takes longer to heat up than metal pots, but once it does it retains the heat much longer and allows you to finish cooking the ingredients with its residual heat. If you live in Los Angeles, check out Toiro for their incredible selection of donabe. (You can also order them from their online store.)

Suribachi and Surikogi すり鉢 / すりこぎ

Suribachi and surikogi is a Japanese mortar and pestle. The ceramic bowl (suribachi) has shallow grooves that create a rough surface that is particularly perfect for catching and grinding sesame seeds. In this book I mainly use suribachi and surikogi for grinding sesame seeds. (If you don't have one, you can grind the seeds by putting them in a resealable plastic bag and crushing them with a rolling pin, or pulsing them in a spice grinder until coarsely ground. You can also use a regular mortar and pestle, but it'll take longer to grind the sesame seeds.) The mortars come in different sizes; I recommend finding one that is about 7 inches in diameter.

vegetables

dashi 出汁
what is dashi?

Dashi is an umami-packed broth that is used liberally in Japanese cooking. It is the base of many recipes, such as Loaded Vegetable Miso Soup (page 34), Oyako Don (chicken and egg rice bowl, page 121), Mini Okonomiyaki (mini cabbage pancakes, page 174), and Inarizushi (page 195). Unlike a classic French stock, which is made with fresh ingredients, dashi is mostly made with dried pantry items, such as katsuobushi (dried and shaved bonito), kombu (dried kelp), niboshi (dried anchovy), and hoshi-shiitake (dried mushrooms). These dried ingredients are very flavorful, so you only need a small amount of each one and a short cooking time. Dashi has a subtle flavor on its own—kombu dashi almost tastes like the ocean without salt, whereas awase dashi has a mild afternote of roasted fish—but when you combine it with other ingredients, it enhances the dish and can completely transform it. I think of dashi almost like a primer for painting. You won't see it, but it is a crucial material for an excellent outcome. Similarly, you may not taste the dashi in a dish the way you would taste a "stronger" flavor, but it'll be integral to melding together the other flavors.

There are many ways of making dashi. In this book, I mainly use awase dashi and kombu dashi. The ingredients needed to make them—kombu and bonito flakes—are easy to find in grocery stores across the US.

Instant dashi is a convenient alternative to making dashi from scratch since it immediately dissolves in water. It's widely used in Japanese households and is available at Asian or Japanese grocery stores and online. Many of my chef friends love it, especially when they need only small amounts of dashi. If you don't have time to make dashi, you can substitute with instant dashi—the dish will be just as delicious. The one exception is my Kitsune Udon (udon in broth with fried tofu, page 153), for which I strongly recommend making dashi from scratch. Most instant dashi contains salt, so make sure to taste it first and adjust the seasoning as needed. There are many kinds of instant dashi, including vegan kombu dashi. Follow the package directions, as each one is a bit different.

how to make dashi at home

Kombu Dashi 昆布だし

Kombu dashi is a great vegan option, as it is only made with water and kombu. You can use it throughout the book whenever a recipe calls for dashi. Its subtle flavor pairs well with everything.

Makes 4 cups

2 (4-inch-square) pieces kombu

1. Using a damp paper towel, gently wipe the kombu. You're just looking to remove any dust or dirt, so there's no need to scrub it clean. If you see a bit of white powder, don't wipe it off.

2. There are two methods for making kombu dashi:

COLD-BREW METHOD: Pour 4 cups water into a large bowl or jar. Add the kombu. Refrigerate for at least 3 hours and up to overnight (10 to 15 hours). You don't want to steep the kombu for too long, otherwise the dashi might take on a fishy smell and become a bit slimy.

STOVETOP METHOD: In a medium pot, combine the kombu and 4 cups water. Soak for at least 30 minutes and up to 1 hour. Set the pot over medium-low heat and heat the mixture for 10 minutes, but do not let it boil. Remove the pot from the heat right before the water begins to boil. If you boil the kombu the dashi might take on a fishy smell and become a bit slimy. Remove the kombu and discard. If you're not using the dashi right away, let it cool to room temperature.

3. Kombu dashi will keep in an airtight container in the refrigerator for up to 3 days, or frozen in an ice cube tray and stored in a resealable plastic bag for up to 3 months.

Awase Dashi 合わせだし

I use awase dashi the most in my cooking. Awase means "combined" in Japanese, so this dashi is made from kombu dashi combined with bonito flakes for an added layer of umami and a smoky aftertaste. I recommend using this dashi for miso soups (pages 34 and 37), Inarizushi (page 195), and Oyako Don (chicken and egg rice bowl, page 121), where you'll taste the difference in flavor the most.

Makes 4 cups

4 cups Kombu Dashi (opposite)

1½ cups (12g) bonito flakes

tip | I like to put the bonito flakes in individual tea bags. Just remove the tea bag, squeeze the excess liquid into the pot, and discard the bag.

1. In a medium pot, bring the kombu dashi to a simmer over medium heat. Turn off the heat and add the bonito flakes to the pot. Turn the heat on low and cook for 3 minutes. Do not stir. Remove the pot from the heat.

2. Line a fine-mesh sieve with a paper towel, cheesecloth, or clean kitchen towel and set it over a large bowl. Strain the dashi and discard the bonito flakes. Don't worry if there are some flakes in the dashi; they are perfectly edible.

3. Awase dashi will keep in an airtight container in the refrigerator for up to 3 days, or frozen in an ice cube tray and stored in a resealable plastic bag for up to 3 months.

Loaded Vegetable Miso Soup

具沢山のお味噌汁

On a cold winter day, many years ago, I was in the vegetable section of a grocery store, craving miso soup. Traditional miso soup is made with very few ingredients (dashi, miso paste, scallions, wakame seaweed, and maybe tofu) and is served as a side dish to complete a meal. I wanted something heartier and filling to warm me up on a winter eve. I decided to add more vegetables to the soup: kabocha and carrot for their sweetness, kale for its bite and texture. The color of lacinato kale reminded me a bit of seaweed, but the sturdy greens provided more heft to the soup. Incredibly nourishing and satisfying, this soup is my "eat-your-vegetables soup" because of how colorful and varied it is. If you can't find kabocha, use an equal amount of sweet potato. Both are velvety and sweet and balance out the saltiness of the miso.

Serves 4 as a side or 2 as a main

¾ pound kabocha squash (about ¼ kabocha)

1 turnip, peeled (about 5 ounces)

4 cups awase or kombu dashi, instant or homemade (see page 32)

1 carrot, cut into ¼-inch rounds (about 1 cup)

½ white or yellow onion, thinly sliced (about 1 cup)

2 ounces shiitake or oyster mushrooms, halved and sliced or torn into ½-inch pieces (about 2 cups)

3 lacinato kale leaves, stemmed and leaves torn into bite-size pieces (about 2 cups)

3 tablespoons miso, plus more to taste

1. Halve the kabocha quarter through the stem into two wedges. Cut each wedge crosswise into ¼-inch-thick slices. You don't need to peel the kabocha; just remove any gnarly bumps with a sharp knife. Cut the turnip into quarters through the stem, then cut each quarter crosswise into ¼-inch-thick slices.

2. In a large pot, combine the kabocha, turnip, dashi, carrot, onion, and mushrooms. Bring to a boil over high heat. Reduce the heat to medium and simmer until the vegetables are tender, 4 to 6 minutes. Add the kale and cover the pot. Cook, covered, until the kale is wilted, 1 to 2 minutes. Remove the pot from the heat.

3. Place the miso in a small bowl. Ladle some hot dashi into the bowl and stir to completely dissolve the miso. Pour the dissolved miso into the pot. Stir to combine, then taste the soup and add more water or miso, as desired.

4. Serve immediately. The soup will keep in an airtight container in the refrigerator for up to overnight. To reheat, gently warm the soup in a pot over low heat, being careful not to boil the miso.

tip | You will only use about a quarter of a kabocha squash for this recipe. To store leftover kabocha, scrape out all the seeds, tightly wrap the squash in plastic, and refrigerate for up to 1 week.

Dango Miso Soup

お団子入り味噌汁

Dango is a rice flour dumpling that is similar in appearance and texture to mochi. However, mochi is made from cooked mochi rice grains that are pounded into a sticky rice cake, whereas dango is made from sweet rice flour. There are two kinds of sweet rice flours, shiratamako and mochiko. In Japan, we use shiratamako to make dango because it yields a silky texture, but it can be hard to find in the US. You can make dango with mochiko, which is more available. Though the texture will be a bit different, the flavor will be just as delicious.

I loved this soup as a child—probably because the dumplings reminded me of dessert. (You will often find dango in Japanese sweets.) I remember helping my mother make dango: She would tear off small pieces for me to shape into balls, and it was almost like playing with Play-Doh.

Serves 4

DANGO

1⅓ cups (164g) shiratamako or 1⅓ cups (200g) mochiko

Pinch of kosher salt

MISO SOUP

4 cups awase or kombu dashi, instant or homemade (see page 32)

1 medium carrot, cut into ¼-inch pieces (about ⅔ cup)

¼ white or yellow onion, thinly sliced (about ½ cup)

1 small Japanese sweet potato or 1 large Yukon Gold potato, peeled and cut into ⅛-inch half-moons (about 1 cup)

3 tablespoons miso, plus more to taste

1. MAKE THE DANGO: In a medium bowl, combine the shiratamako and salt. While mixing with chopsticks or a fork, gradually add ⅔ cup water, 1 tablespoon at a time, until the dough starts to come together in large crumbles, almost like feta cheese. Add more water, a sprinkle at a time, and bring the dough together with your hands. Knead the dough until it forms a smooth ball.

2. Roll the dough into 1-inch balls (scant 1 tablespoon) and gently press to slightly flatten. The dango should be about 1¼ inches in diameter and ½ inch thick. Use your finger to press the center to make a dent; this will help them cook evenly. You should have about 20 dango. Cover with a damp paper towel and set aside.

3. MAKE THE MISO SOUP: In a medium pot, combine the dashi, carrot, onion, and sweet potato. Bring to a boil over high heat. Reduce the heat to medium and simmer until the vegetables are tender, 3 to 5 minutes.

4. Add the dango and cook until they float to the surface and are a bit translucent, about 3 minutes. Remove the pot from the heat.

5. Place the miso in a small bowl. Ladle some dashi into the bowl and stir to completely dissolve the miso. Add the dissolved miso to the pot and stir to combine. Taste the soup and add more water or miso, as desired.

6. Serve immediately. The soup will keep in an airtight container in the refrigerator for up to overnight. To reheat, warm the soup in a pot over low heat, being careful not to boil the miso.

tip | When you make the dango, add the water gradually and adjust the amount of water as needed. It should feel like Play-Doh. My mom would describe the texture as being "soft as an earlobe."

Soy Sauce-Simmered Kabocha

かぼちゃの煮物

I'm so glad that kabocha is more widely available in American grocery stores, because in my opinion, it's the best variety of squash. It's sweet and less watery compared to other squashes or pumpkins. I love the dense, velvety texture of its flesh, and although the skin looks tough, it's entirely edible. The simmering technique in this recipe, called nimono in Japanese, is similar to gentle braising. If you boil the kabocha, it'll disintegrate around the edges, so I like to use a parchment cartouche to help maintain the shape of the kabocha and enhance its natural sweetness. You can use any leftover raw kabocha to make Loaded Vegetable Miso Soup (page 34) or Curried Kabocha Croquettes (page 46).

Serves 4

1½ pounds kabocha (about ½ kabocha)

1 tablespoon sugar

1 tablespoon soy sauce

¼ teaspoon kosher salt

1. Remove the seeds from the kabocha half. Cut the squash into quarters through the stem, then cut each quarter in half crosswise. If there are any gnarly bumps on the skin, remove them with a sharp knife.

2. Prepare a cartouche (see page 23) the size of a deep medium skillet or shallow pot. In the skillet, combine the kabocha and 1½ cups water. Bring to a simmer over medium heat, using a spoon or mesh skimmer to skim off any impurities that rise to the surface. Add

the sugar and simmer, stirring, until dissolved, about 2 minutes. Add the soy sauce and salt and stir to combine. Reduce the heat to medium-low, place the parchment cartouche on top, and cook until the liquid is almost entirely absorbed and the kabocha is soft enough to be pierced with a toothpick or fork, about 15 minutes.

3. Serve warm. The kabocha and braising liquid will keep in an airtight container in the refrigerator for up to 3 days.

Roasted Cauliflower Goma-ae

カリフラワーの胡麻和え

This sesame-dressed vegetable side dish, called goma-ae, is traditionally made with blanched spinach, but you can use almost any vegetable, such as green beans or broccoli. For my version, I roasted cauliflower in the oven until crispy and starting to caramelize. I love how those concentrated flavors complement the sweet-salty sesame seed dressing. To grind the sesame seeds, I use a Japanese mortar and pestle called suribachi and surikogi, designed especially for this task. The ceramic bowl has shallow grooves that create a rough surface, perfect for catching and grinding the sesame seeds.

Serves 4

3 tablespoons toasted white sesame seeds, coarsely ground (see Tip)

2 tablespoons soy sauce

1 tablespoon sugar

1 medium head cauliflower, cut into florets (about 2 pounds)

2 tablespoons toasted sesame oil

1. Preheat the oven to 425°F. Line a sheet pan with parchment paper.

2. In a small bowl, combine the ground sesame seeds, soy sauce, and sugar. Set aside while the cauliflower roasts, but stir from time to time to dissolve the sugar.

3. In a large bowl, toss the cauliflower with the sesame oil to evenly coat. Spread the cauliflower on the prepared pan. Roast until tender and golden brown at the edges, 20 to 25 minutes.

4. Transfer the cauliflower to a large bowl and add the sesame dressing, tossing to evenly coat. Serve immediately.

tip | Here is how to grind sesame seeds: Place the sesame seeds into a suribachi. Using a surikogi, grind the sesame seeds until coarsely ground, leaving some seeds whole. The sesame seeds will release some oil and a nutty aroma. (Alternatively, put the sesame seeds in a resealable plastic bag and crush with a rolling pin, or pulse in a spice grinder until coarsely ground. You can also use a regular mortar and pestle, but it will take longer to grind the sesame seeds.)

Fried Eggplant
with Miso Sauce

揚げなすの味噌だれ

I think my love of eggplant started with this recipe. Whenever I visited my parents and my mom asked me what I wanted to eat for dinner, I would request fried eggplant with miso. The miso sauce is salty and sweet, and pairs perfectly with the silky fried eggplant. It's also a no-cook sauce—you just stir together the ingredients to dissolve the sugar—so the only real cooking is shallow-frying the eggplant. This dish is particularly delicious and satisfying in the summertime when eggplant is in season.

Serves 4

4 Japanese or Chinese eggplant

1 teaspoon kosher salt

2 tablespoons soy sauce

1 teaspoon rice vinegar

1 teaspoon toasted sesame oil

1 teaspoon miso

1½ tablespoons sugar

2 tablespoons toasted white sesame seeds, coarsely ground (see Tip, page 41)

Neutral oil, such as canola or grapeseed, for shallow-frying

Freshly cooked rice (see page 115), for serving

1. Quarter the eggplant lengthwise, then cut crosswise into 2-inch lengths. Put the eggplant in a medium bowl and sprinkle with the salt. Toss to evenly coat. Set aside for 10 minutes.

2. In a small bowl, combine the soy sauce, rice vinegar, sesame oil, miso, and sugar. Mix well until the miso and sugar are completely dissolved. Stir in the sesame seeds. Set aside.

3. Pour about 1 inch of oil into a medium skillet. Heat the oil over medium heat until hot. Dip a wooden chopstick into the oil; if bubbles immediately form, the oil is hot enough. Using paper towels or a cloth, wipe excess moisture from the eggplant (this will prevent the oil from splattering too much). Line a sheet pan with paper towels, then set a wire rack on top.

4. Working in batches, fry the eggplant, flipping halfway through, until golden, 2 to 3 minutes per side. Transfer the eggplant to the wire rack to drain.

5. Serve the eggplant with the miso sauce for dipping and use the rice for catching the eggplant and sauce. I like to alternate bites of eggplant dipped in sauce and rice.

tips | Like a sponge, eggplant can absorb a lot of oil. If you first sprinkle the eggplant with salt, you can extract some of the moisture and change the structure of the flesh, so it will take in less oil.

• I like using Japanese or Chinese eggplant because their skins are more tender than Italian eggplant—and they're smaller, too.

tips | To prevent too much gluten from developing, make sure the ingredients are cold and don't overmix when making the batter.

• To make ice water, fill a measuring cup with ice and add cold water. Scoop out tablespoons of ice water as needed. (Be careful not to add pieces of ice to the batter.)

• If your carrots don't have tops, you can replace them with 1 cup tender herbs or alliums, such as parsley, dill, basil, chives, and scallions. Pick the leaves from the herbs or coarsely chop the chives and scallions. You can mix and match the herbs depending on what you already have in your fridge.

Carrot Top Tempura

人参の葉っぱのてんぷら

Mottainai is a Japanese term that describes the feeling of not wanting to waste anything, such as food, objects, or time. Whenever I'm about to throw out the tops of vegetables, I feel mottainai. As a result, I try to always find a use for the leafy greens that are often trimmed from vegetables like carrots, radishes, beets, and turnips. Carrot tops have an herb-y flavor that I like, and naturally they pair nicely with the carrots themselves. You could also make this tempura with just carrot tops and onions if you're using the carrots for another recipe. The greens have a similar texture to parsley and get very crisp when fried. You could serve this dish as part of a vegetarian meal with the Cucumber and Fennel Sunomono (page 53), Dango Miso Soup (page 37), and a bowl of rice.

Serves 4

FILLING

4 carrots (about 6 ounces) with their tops

1 small yellow onion, thinly sliced (about 1½ cups)

BATTER

3 tablespoons all-purpose flour

3 tablespoons potato starch or cornstarch

½ teaspoon kosher salt

1 large egg

6 tablespoons ice water (see Tip)

TO FINISH

Neutral oil, such as canola or grapeseed, for shallow-frying

Flaky sea salt, such as Maldon, for sprinkling

1. MAKE THE FILLING: Separate the carrots from the leafy tops. Pick the leaves from the carrot tops, discarding any thick stems. You should have about 1 cup carrot tops. Wash the carrot tops (if they are very gritty, wash them the way you would salad greens: Soak for a few minutes and allow the dirt or grit to sink to the bottom, then lift up the greens with your hand and dry in a salad spinner or with a towel).

2. Using a vegetable peeler, peel the carrots and discard just the top layer (skin). Continue peeling the carrots, rotating as you peel, to make ribbons.

3. In a medium bowl, toss the carrot tops, carrot ribbons, and onion to combine and set aside in the refrigerator.

4. MAKE THE BATTER: Sift the flour and potato starch into a small bowl. Stir in the kosher salt and set aside in the refrigerator. In another small bowl, mix the egg and ice water. Set aside in the refrigerator.

5. Sprinkle 2 tablespoons of the flour mixture over the vegetables. Using chopsticks or a fork, gently toss to evenly coat. Pour the egg mixture and the remaining flour mixture over the vegetables. Toss to coat with the batter, being careful not to overmix.

6. TO FINISH: Line a sheet pan with paper towels and top with a wire rack. Pour about 1 inch of oil into a large deep pot or a Dutch oven. Heat the oil over medium-high heat until it registers 350°F on a deep-fry thermometer.

7. Working in batches, use a large spoon to scoop out about ½ cup of the vegetable mixture and gently drop it into the oil. Use a second spoon or chopsticks to push the mixture into the oil. Cook until golden, 2 to 4 minutes. Flip and cook on the other side until golden brown, 2 to 4 minutes more. Transfer the tempura to the wire rack and immediately sprinkle with the sea salt. Repeat with the remaining batter.

8. Serve hot or at room temperature.

Curried Kabocha Croquettes

かぼちゃのコロッケ

Japanese croquettes, known as korokke, are usually made with mashed potatoes and ground beef. They're very common in Japan—you can even find prepared ones at the butcher. For a vegetarian option, I love using kabocha. It has a smooth, velvety texture that makes for a creamy filling that contrasts beautifully with the crisp shell. I was inspired by a friend's curried kabocha soup and added curry powder for some lingering spice. Since the filling is already cooked, you only need to shallow-fry them for just a few minutes to brown the panko.

I know making croquettes from scratch is a labor of love, but I think they're absolutely worth the effort. Leftover croquettes can be eaten at room temperature in a bento (my personal favorite) or reheated in the oven until warm.

Makes about 16 croquettes (serves 4)

⅓ kabocha, peeled and cut into 1-inch pieces (about 3 cups; 14 ounces)

1 tablespoon unsalted butter

1 cup finely chopped yellow onion (about ½ onion)

Kosher salt

1¼ teaspoons curry powder

1 large egg

3 tablespoons all-purpose flour

1½ cups panko bread crumbs

2 tablespoons black sesame seeds (optional)

Neutral oil, such as canola or grapeseed, for shallow-frying

1. Cook the kabocha squash using one of the methods below until it can be easily pierced with a toothpick or fork:

SIMMER: Place the kabocha in a large pot. Add enough water to just cover the kabocha. Bring to a simmer and cook until soft, 10 to 15 minutes.

STEAM: Fill a large pot with 2 inches of water and fit with a steamer basket. Add the kabocha to the basket, cover the pot with a lid, and bring to a boil. Steam, covered, until the kabocha is soft, 10 to 15 minutes.

MICROWAVE: In a microwave-safe bowl, combine the kabocha and 1 tablespoon of water. Cover with plastic wrap, making sure to leave one edge uncovered by about 1 inch, so the steam can escape. Microwave until the kabocha is soft, 5 to 10 minutes. (The cooking time will depend on your microwave.) Remove the plastic wrap, being careful not to burn your fingers with the hot steam.

2. Using a slotted spoon, transfer the kabocha to a large bowl and mash with a potato masher or a fork. Set aside.

3. In a medium skillet, melt the butter over medium-low heat. Add the onion and season with ¼ teaspoon salt. Cook, stirring, until soft and translucent, about 8 minutes. Add the curry powder and cook, stirring, for 2 minutes.

4. Transfer the cooked onion to the bowl with the kabocha. Add 1 teaspoon salt and stir well to combine.

5. Using your hands, shape the kabocha mixture into balls the size of golf balls (about 2 tablespoons each). If the kabocha mixture sticks to your hands, wet your hands. You should have about 16 balls. Set aside.

6. In a medium bowl, whisk the egg with 2 tablespoons water. (Make sure there are no visible egg white streaks.)

Add the flour and whisk to combine. Set aside.

7. Place the panko and sesame seeds (if using) in a shallow dish. Stir to combine.

8. Working one at a time, dip the kabocha balls into the egg mixture, allowing any excess to drain. Roll the balls in the panko mixture to evenly coat and put them on a large plate.

9. Pour about 1 inch of oil into a cast-iron skillet or medium skillet. Heat the oil over medium-high heat until hot. To check the temperature of the oil, add a few crumbs of panko. They should immediately sizzle. You can also dip a wooden chopstick into the oil and see if bubbles form around the chopstick.

10. Line a large plate with paper towels. Working in batches, cook the croquettes, turning several times, until golden brown all over, about 6 minutes. Transfer the croquettes to the paper towels to drain.

11. Serve hot or at room temperature. The croquettes will keep in an airtight container in the refrigerator for up to 3 days.

Broccoli and Bean Salad

ブロッコリーといんげんのサラダ

This hearty salad is a substantial, filling vegetable side that can be dressed several hours in advance since the sturdy broccoli and green beans won't wilt. If anything, they will absorb more of the dressing over time. Just make sure to toss again before serving. For this salad dressing, I like using whole-grain mustard, as it gives a nice pop. I've also incorporated staple Japanese ingredients—soy sauce, rice vinegar, and sesame oil—to provide extra depth of flavor. The dressing pairs well with other vegetables, such as shredded cabbage, blanched cauliflower, and sugar snap peas. Try to find green beans that haven't been pretrimmed. I prefer to cook the beans whole, so that they don't absorb too much water and retain their crisp bite.

Serves 4

DRESSING

3 tablespoons toasted sesame oil

1 tablespoon whole-grain mustard

1 tablespoon soy sauce

1 tablespoon rice vinegar

½ teaspoon kosher salt

1 garlic clove, finely grated

SALAD

Kosher salt

1 head broccoli (about 9 ounces), cut into florets and stem sliced ⅛ inch thick

6 ounces green beans

1 (15-ounce) can chickpeas or cannellini beans, drained and rinsed

1. MAKE THE DRESSING: In a small bowl, combine the sesame oil, mustard, soy sauce, rice vinegar, salt, and garlic. Using a fork or small whisk, mix until well combined. The dressing will keep in an airtight container in the refrigerator for up to 2 days.

2. MAKE THE SALAD: Bring a large pot of salted water to a boil. Add the broccoli and cook for 2 minutes. Using a slotted spoon, transfer the broccoli to a medium bowl.

3. Add the green beans to the boiling water and cook for 2 minutes. Drain the green beans and rinse under cold water. Pat dry. Using a sharp knife, trim and discard the ends of the green beans, then cut the beans on a diagonal into 2-inch pieces. Add to the bowl with the broccoli. Add the chickpeas and toss to combine.

4. Drizzle the dressing over the vegetables and beans and stir to combine. The salad will keep in an airtight container in the refrigerator for up to 5 hours.

Potato Salad

ポテトサラダ

Japanese potato salad often features fruit, such as apples or canned mandarins, and is a little creamier and less vinegary than American potato salad. The luscious texture comes from Kewpie mayo, a Japanese brand of mayonnaise that has become more popular in the US and is increasingly available at grocery stores around the country. (It's also available online.) Unlike regular American mayonnaise, Kewpie is made with only egg yolks, so it has a richer, eggy flavor. Some recipes for Japanese potato salad call for sugar, but I like adding apple and find it lends the right amount of sweetness. If you don't like fruit in your salads, you can skip it.

Serves 4

2 russet potatoes (about 1 pound), peeled and cut into 2-inch pieces

Kosher salt

1 Persian (mini) cucumber, cut into ⅛-inch slices (about 1 cup)

½ sweet or white onion, thinly sliced (about 1½ cups)

½ Fuji apple, halved, cored, and thinly sliced (about 1 cup)

5 tablespoons Kewpie mayonnaise

2 teaspoons rice vinegar or apple cider vinegar

Freshly ground black pepper

1. Fill a large pot with water and add the potatoes and 1 teaspoon salt. Bring to a boil over high heat. Reduce the heat to medium and cook until the potatoes can be easily pierced with a toothpick or fork, 10 to 15 minutes. Drain the potatoes, return them to the pot, and set the pot over medium heat. Cook, stirring, until the potatoes are dry, about 1 minute.

2. Roughly mash the potatoes with a fork, potato masher, or rice paddle. Almost half of the potatoes should be mashed, leaving the rest in whole pieces. Transfer to a large bowl and set aside.

3. In a medium bowl, combine the cucumber and onion and sprinkle with ½ teaspoon salt. Set aside for 5 minutes. Using your hands, squeeze as much liquid as possible out of the vegetables, then add them to the potatoes.

4. Add the apple, mayonnaise, and rice vinegar to the bowl. Season with salt and pepper. Stir well to combine. Taste and season with more salt and pepper, if needed. Serve at room temperature. The potato salad will keep in an airtight container in the refrigerator for up to 3 days.

tip | Potato salad is usually served as a small side to complement a meal, so you'll just need about ½ cup per person. One of my favorite ways to eat potato salad is for breakfast: Toast a slice of bread and top it with cold leftover potato salad, straight from the fridge. I love the combination of crisp warm bread and soft cold potatoes.

Cucumber and Fennel Sunomono

きゅうりとフェンネルの酢の物

This vinegary vegetable side dish is very refreshing and easy to make. It reminds me of a palate cleanser and is the perfect small side to balance a richer meal, such as the Ginger Pork Chops (page 78), Karaage (page 62), or Curried Kabocha Croquettes (page 46). There are many ways to make sunomono, the simplest version being with cucumber. I've added fennel for a hint of anise. The dressing has no oil and is made with just vinegar, salt, and sugar. The sugar is an important ingredient, as it counters the sharpness of the vinegar. I recommend starting with 1 teaspoon of sugar, tasting the dressing, and adding more to your liking.

Serves 4

1 English cucumber, very thinly sliced (about 3 cups)

Kosher salt

½ fennel bulb, very thinly sliced (about 1 cup)

¼ cup rice vinegar

1 teaspoon sugar, plus more to taste

2 tablespoons toasted white sesame seeds, whole or coarsely ground (see Tip, page 41)

1. Place the cucumber in a medium bowl and sprinkle it with 1 teaspoon salt. Toss to combine. Set aside for 10 minutes. Drain the cucumber, using your hands to squeeze out more liquid.

2. Add the fennel to the bowl with the cucumber. Stir to combine.

tip | I highly recommend using a mandoline to slice the cucumber and fennel. It's the easiest and quickest way to get thin, uniform slices. Be careful with it! If you don't have a mandoline, use a sharp knife and make sure the slices are about 1/16 inch thick.

3. In a small bowl, combine the rice vinegar, sugar, and ¼ teaspoon salt. Stir well to completely dissolve the sugar and salt. Taste and add more sugar if desired. Stir in the ground sesame seeds.

4. Drizzle the vinegar mixture over the cucumber and fennel. Stir to evenly coat the vegetables. Serve immediately. The cucumber and fennel salad will keep in an airtight container in the refrigerator for up to 2 days.

Cabbage Salad
with Lemon-Miso Dressing
せん切りキャベツのサラダ

If you go to a tonkatsu (fried pork cutlet) restaurant in Japan, your order of tonkatsu will come with a mountain of shredded cabbage, and often you get free refills of cabbage. My mom would always keep in the fridge a container of thinly sliced cabbage mixed in with other vegetables, such as carrots and onions, to use whenever she wanted a side salad. All the vegetables for this salad should be sliced very thinly to better catch the dressing. I especially love pairing cabbage with this lemon-miso dressing, but you could also make a simple mustard vinaigrette or any other dressing you like.

Serves 4

LEMON-MISO DRESSING

2 tablespoons Lemon Miso (recipe follows)

2 tablespoons rice vinegar

¼ cup extra-virgin olive oil

Kosher salt and freshly ground black pepper

CABBAGE SALAD

¼ head green cabbage (about 10 ounces)

½ white or sweet onion (optional), thinly sliced

1 Persian (mini) cucumber (optional), thinly sliced

1 carrot (optional), cut into thin matchsticks or grated

3 radishes (optional), thinly sliced

1. MAKE THE LEMON-MISO DRESSING: In a small bowl, combine the lemon miso and rice vinegar. Whisk well to dissolve the lemon miso completely. Drizzle in the oil and whisk until smooth and combined. Season with salt and pepper. (Alternatively, combine all the ingredients in a jar with a lid and shake until smooth and combined.) The dressing will keep in an airtight container in the refrigerator for up to 4 days.

2. MAKE THE CABBAGE SALAD: Remove the core from the cabbage. Roll up the leaves and slice very thinly. (If using a mandoline, do not remove the core and slice very thinly.) Fill a large bowl with cold water and place the sliced cabbage in the water. Soak for 5 minutes, then drain and pat dry or spin in a salad spinner. Place the cabbage in a large bowl.

3. If using the onion, soak the slices in cold water for 5 minutes. Drain and pat dry. Add to the large bowl.

4. Add any of the following optional ingredients you are using: cucumber, carrot, or radishes. Toss to mix everything together. The vegetables will keep in a container lined with paper towels (see Tip) in the refrigerator for up to 3 days.

5. When ready to serve, drizzle the dressing on the cabbage and toss to combine.

tip | Keep the sliced cabbage in a container lined with paper towels and cover with a damp paper towel. The dry paper towels catch excess moisture from the cabbage and the damp paper towel keeps it from completely drying out.

(recipe continues)

Lemon Miso
レモン味噌

This lemon miso is inspired by yuzu miso, a sweet-salty citrusy miso commonly found in Japan. It's a very versatile ingredient that pairs beautifully with fish, crudités, and salad dressings. I wanted to re-create a similar miso paste, but yuzu is hard to find in the US. Since I have a lemon tree in my backyard, I started experimenting with lemons. With sweet honey mellowing out the saltiness of the miso, this lemon miso is as vibrant and delicious as yuzu miso.

Makes about ½ cup

5 tablespoons miso

2 tablespoons mirin

2 tablespoons honey

2 tablespoons fresh lemon juice

1 teaspoon grated lemon zest

1. In a small saucepan, combine the miso and mirin. Cook over medium-low heat, stirring often, until the mixture is smooth, 1 to 3 minutes. (This will evaporate some of the alcohol from the mirin.) Remove the pan from the heat and stir in the honey, lemon juice, and lemon zest.

2. Transfer to a sterilized jar (see Tip on page 126) and seal tightly. The lemon miso will keep in the refrigerator for up to 1 week.

Green Salad with Umeboshi Dressing

グリーンサラダと梅干しのドレッシング

There's an expression in Japanese—natsu bate—to describe the feeling of losing your appetite in the summer because it's really hot. We say that umeboshi (pickled plum; see page 22) is one of the ingredients that can bring back your appetite. In fact, just thinking about umeboshi makes my mouth water. It's very sour and alkaline, and also has medicinal properties—it's recommended for when you have an upset stomach or feel nauseous. Umeboshi is often used as a filling for onigiri (rice balls), as its intense flavor marries well with plain white rice. It's somewhat of an acquired taste and is quite salty on its own, so you probably won't need to add salt to this dressing, but taste it and see what you think. You can play around with the vegetables in this salad. Use whatever is available, such as lettuce, cucumber, and avocado. If rhubarb is in season, I recommend making the Salted Rhubarb Paste (recipe follows). The idea came from a Japanese friend, and it really does taste just like umeboshi.

Serves 4

UMEBOSHI DRESSING

1 tablespoon umeboshi paste or Salted Rhubarb Paste (recipe follows)

2 tablespoons rice vinegar

¼ teaspoon honey

¼ cup plus 2 tablespoons extra-virgin olive oil

SALAD

5 asparagus stalks, woody ends trimmed

1 cup sugar snap peas, stems and strings removed

Kosher salt

5 radishes, quartered

1 head butter lettuce, torn into bite-size pieces

1. MAKE THE UMEBOSHI DRESSING: Place the umeboshi paste in a small bowl. Add 1 tablespoon water and whisk well. Add the rice vinegar and honey and whisk to combine. Slowly drizzle in the olive oil, whisking constantly, until smooth and combined. The dressing will keep in an airtight container in the refrigerator for up to 1 week.

2. MAKE THE SALAD: Cut the asparagus into 1-inch pieces. Cut the sugar snap peas on a diagonal into ¼-inch slices.

3. Bring a medium pot of salted water to a boil. Add the asparagus and cook for 2 minutes. Drain and rinse under cold water.

4. In a large bowl, combine the asparagus, sugar snap peas, radishes, and butter lettuce. Drizzle the dressing over the salad and toss to coat.

tips | If you can't find umeboshi paste, use 1 to 3 whole umeboshi (umeboshi vary in size) to end up with 1 tablespoon paste. Remove the pit(s) and place on a cutting board. Gently mash with the back of a knife to make a paste. Measure out 1 tablespoon.

• To freeze rhubarb, cut into 1-inch pieces and store in a resealable plastic bag.

(recipe continues)

Salted Rhubarb Paste
ルバーブの塩煮

Makes a heaping ½ cup

½ pound rhubarb, cut into 1-inch pieces (fresh or frozen)

2 teaspoons kosher salt

1 teaspoon sumac

1. Place the rhubarb in a medium saucepan. Sprinkle with the salt. Using a rubber spatula, mix well to evenly coat the rhubarb in salt. Set aside for 30 minutes. The rhubarb will release some liquid.

2. Add 2 teaspoons water to the rhubarb. (No need to add the water if the rhubarb is frozen.) Cook over medium heat, stirring constantly and breaking up the rhubarb with the spatula, until it forms a thick paste, 10 to 15 minutes. The rhubarb should be mostly broken down with a few small visible pieces.

3. Remove the pan from the heat and stir in the sumac. Transfer to a jar or an airtight container and let cool to room temperature. The salted rhubarb paste will keep in an airtight container in the refrigerator for up to 1 week, or wrap small portions (about 1 tablespoon) in plastic and freeze for up to 3 months.

meat

62
Karaage

65
Sweet Soy Sauce
Chicken Wings

66
Sweet and Sour Chicken
with Balsamic Vinegar Sauce

69
Chicken-Tofu Tsukune

70
Spicy Chicken Salad

73
Curry Rice

75
Rib-Eye Steak
with Shoyu-Garlic Sauce

78
Ginger Pork Chops

80
Chā Shū

82
Nikujaga

84
Tamagoyaki

87
Tonkatsu

Karaage

鶏のからあげ

For karaage (Japanese fried chicken), you first marinate the chicken in a flavorful sweet and salty sauce. The subtle sweetness comes from mirin, and there's some lingering heat from ginger and garlic. Instead of dredging in flour, I use potato starch for a thin, crispy shell that binds perfectly to the chicken. The pieces should be bite-size, so they can be easily eaten with chopsticks or fit into a bento box. It might seem unusual to put fried chicken in a bento box, but I promise it's delicious served cold or at room temperature.

I recommend serving karaage with a bowl of white rice or Corn Rice (page 134) and a vegetable side, such as the Soy Sauce–Simmered Kabocha (page 38).

Serves 4

1½ pounds boneless, skinless chicken thighs, cut into 2-inch pieces

2 tablespoons soy sauce

2 tablespoons mirin

2 tablespoons sake

1 tablespoon toasted sesame oil

1 teaspoon finely grated fresh ginger

1 garlic clove, finely grated

1 cup potato starch or cornstarch

Neutral oil, such as canola or grapeseed, for frying

Lemon wedges, for serving

1. Place the chicken in a large bowl or resealable plastic bag.

2. In a small bowl, whisk the soy sauce, mirin, sake, sesame oil, ginger, and garlic. Pour the mixture onto the chicken. If using a bowl, gently toss the chicken with the marinade to evenly coat. If using a resealable plastic bag, close the bag and gently massage the marinade into the chicken to evenly distribute. Cover and refrigerate for at least 1 hour and up to overnight.

3. Drain the chicken in a sieve and discard the marinade. Place the chicken in a large bowl and sprinkle with the potato starch. Toss to evenly coat each piece.

4. Pour 1½ inches of oil into a large deep pot or Dutch oven. Heat the oil over medium heat until it registers 320°F on a deep-fry thermometer.

5. Set a wire rack in a sheet pan and line a large plate with paper towels. Working in batches, fry the chicken until pale golden and cooked through,

3 to 4 minutes. Transfer the chicken to the wire rack.

6. Increase the heat to medium-high and heat the oil to 360°F. Working in batches, fry the chicken a second time until golden brown, 1 to 3 minutes. The chicken should be cooked through and the outside crispy. Transfer to the paper towels to drain.

7. Serve immediately with lemon wedges for squeezing.

tips | If you have time, make this recipe with boneless, skin-on chicken thighs. Start with bone-in, skin-on chicken thighs and remove the bone using a sharp knife. The fried skin adds another layer of crunchiness and flavor.

• This recipe calls for double frying, the technique used in Sweet Soy Sauce Chicken Wings (page 65). First you fry at a lower temperature to cook the chicken, then again at a higher temperature to achieve that beautiful golden-brown shell.

Sweet Soy Sauce Chicken Wings

手羽先の甘辛風

My mother would make chicken legs with this sweet soy glaze for special occasions. I adapted her recipe for chicken wings for Tasty's fried chicken cook-off at BuzzFeed. The recipe was such a hit that my co-workers often request it for birthdays, farewell parties, and other celebratory occasions. The ingredient amounts for the glaze can easily be multiplied to feed a crowd, just make sure to follow the ratio of 2:1:1:1 (2 parts soy sauce to 1 part each mirin, sake, and sugar).

This recipe calls for a double-frying method that yields tender, fall-off-the-bone meat and a crunchy, satisfying shell. First you fry the wings over low heat to cook the chicken through, then you fry at a higher temperature to get that perfect crispy texture on the outside.

Serves 4 as a main
and 6 as an appetizer

**SWEET SOY
SAUCE GLAZE**

1 cup soy sauce

½ cup mirin

½ cup sake

½ cup sugar

2 garlic cloves,
finely grated

CHICKEN WINGS

Neutral oil, such as canola
or grapeseed, for frying

3½ pounds chicken wings,
wing tips removed, split
into flats and drumettes

Kosher salt and freshly
ground black pepper

Potato starch or
cornstarch, for dredging
(about 1½ cups)

Toasted white sesame
seeds, for serving

1. MAKE THE SWEET SOY SAUCE GLAZE: In a large skillet, combine the soy sauce, mirin, sake, sugar, and garlic. Bring to a simmer over medium-high heat and cook, stirring, until the glaze is thick and coats the back of a spoon, 3 to 4 minutes. The glaze will keep in an airtight container in the refrigerator for 2 weeks. Warm it over low heat before coating the chicken.

2. COOK THE CHICKEN WINGS: Pour 1½ inches of oil into a large deep pot or Dutch oven. Heat the oil over medium heat until it registers 320°F on a deep-fry thermometer.

3. Season the chicken wings all over with salt and pepper. Place the potato starch in a large shallow bowl. Dredge the chicken wings in potato starch to evenly coat.

4. Set a wire rack in a sheet pan. Line another sheet pan or large tray with paper towels. Working in batches, fry the wings until pale golden and cooked through, about 7 minutes. Transfer the chicken wings to the wire rack.

5. Increase the heat to medium-high and heat the oil to 350°F. Working in batches, fry the chicken wings a second time until golden brown, about 3 minutes. Transfer the chicken wings to the paper towels to drain.

6. Add the chicken wings to the glaze and toss to evenly coat. Sprinkle with the sesame seeds and serve immediately.

tip | When you first add the chicken to the hot oil, the oil bubbles will be big and loud. When the chicken is cooked through, the bubbles will be smaller and less loud. In Japan, we say it sounds like the pitter-patter of rain.

Sweet and Sour Chicken
with Balsamic Vinegar Sauce
鶏と野菜のバルサミコ酢あん

This recipe is inspired by a chicken and black vinegar dish from Ootoya, a restaurant I loved going to for a quick lunch when I worked in Tokyo. It comes with lotus root and is served in their teishoku set (rice, miso soup, pickles, and one protein side). I miss this dish so much that I re-create it at home. If you find lotus root, try it instead of the carrot for a refreshing crunch.

Serves 4

1 pound boneless, skinless chicken thighs, cut into 1½-inch cubes

2 tablespoons sake

4 tablespoons soy sauce

2 garlic cloves, finely grated

2 teaspoons finely grated fresh ginger

½ cup plus 1 teaspoon potato starch or cornstarch

½ cup neutral oil, such as canola or grapeseed

1 medium carrot, cut into 1-inch pieces

½ yellow onion, cut into ¼-inch-thick slices

¼ cup balsamic vinegar

2 tablespoons sugar

2 tablespoons mirin

1 small yellow or red bell pepper, cut into ½-inch pieces (about ¾ cup)

Freshly cooked rice (see page 115), for serving

1. In a large bowl or a resealable plastic bag, combine the chicken, sake, 2 tablespoons of the soy sauce, the garlic, and ginger. Mix well and refrigerate for at least 10 minutes and up to 12 hours.

2. Drain the chicken in a sieve and discard the marinade. Transfer the chicken to a medium bowl. Sprinkle ½ cup of the potato starch over the chicken, evenly coating each piece.

3. Line a large plate with paper towels. In a medium skillet with a lid, heat the oil over medium-high heat. When it starts to shimmer, add the chicken in one layer and fry until golden brown, about 3 minutes. Flip the chicken and cook on the other side until golden brown and crispy, about 3 minutes more. Transfer the chicken to the paper towels to drain.

4. To the skillet, add the carrot and cook, stirring occasionally, until golden brown, 3 to 5 minutes. Transfer to the plate with the chicken. Carefully pour out the excess oil from the skillet into a heatproof bowl. Let the oil cool completely, then discard.

5. To the skillet, add the onion and cook, stirring, until softened, 2 to 3 minutes. Return the cooked chicken and carrots to the skillet. Add the balsamic vinegar, sugar, mirin, remaining 2 tablespoons soy sauce, and ¼ cup water. Bring to a boil and reduce the heat to medium. Cover the skillet and cook at a gentle simmer, stirring occasionally, until the sauce is reduced by one-third, about 5 minutes.

6. In a small bowl, combine the remaining 1 teaspoon potato starch with 2 teaspoons water, stirring to make a slurry. Add the bell pepper to the skillet and stir well. Add the slurry and cook, stirring constantly, until thickened, about 2 minutes.

7. Serve hot with a bowl of rice on the side.

Chicken-Tofu Tsukune

鶏のつくね

For these chicken tsukune (meatballs), I use tofu to bind the ingredients instead of soaked bread or bread crumbs. In Japan it's common to mix in tofu with other ingredients as it's more affordable than meat and considered healthier. Since tofu is mild in flavor, it doesn't affect the taste of a dish. It also gives the meatballs a lovely soft texture and adds moisture to the chicken. I like to eat the meatballs dipped in raw egg yolk, but if you're worried about eating raw egg, you can try a poached egg. Serve the meatballs with a bowl of rice and the Potato Salad (page 50) or Cucumber and Fennel Sunomono (page 53).

Serves 4

SWEET SOY SAUCE

2 tablespoons soy sauce

2 tablespoons sake

2 tablespoons mirin

1 tablespoon plus
1 teaspoon sugar

MEATBALLS

8 ounces firm tofu

1 pound ground chicken

2 scallions, finely chopped

2 tablespoons potato
starch or cornstarch

1 teaspoon kosher salt

½ teaspoon freshly
ground black pepper

2 tablespoons neutral
oil, such as canola or
grapeseed

Toasted white sesame
seeds, for garnish

1. MAKE THE SWEET SOY SAUCE: In a small bowl, combine the soy sauce, sake, mirin, and sugar. Whisk until the sugar is completely dissolved. Set aside.

2. MAKE THE MEATBALLS: Place the tofu on a plate lined with paper towels. Set aside for 10 minutes and gently press to remove excess water.

3. Transfer the tofu to a medium bowl. Using your hands, a whisk, or a potato masher, break apart the tofu and mash until finely broken down. The texture should be similar to ground meat.

4. Add the ground chicken to the tofu and mix until fully combined and sticky. The mixture should hold together. Add the scallions, potato starch, salt, and pepper. Mix well until fully combined.

5. Shape the meatball mixture into large balls (about 3 tablespoons per meatball). If the mixture sticks to your hands, lightly wet your hands with water. Sightly flatten the meatballs to a 1-inch thickness. You should have 14 to 16 meatballs.

6. In a large cast-iron pan or nonstick skillet, heat the oil over medium heat. Working in batches, cook the meatballs until golden brown, about 2 minutes per side. Reduce the heat to low, cover, and cook until the meatballs are cooked through, 5 to 7 minutes. Transfer the meatballs to a plate.

7. Wipe the skillet clean with a paper towel. Add the sweet soy sauce and bring to a simmer over medium-high heat. Cook until the sauce is thick and syrupy, about 2 minutes. Return the meatballs to the skillet and coat with the sauce. Sprinkle with sesame seeds, if desired, and serve immediately.

Spicy Chicken Salad

よだれ鶏サラダ

This recipe is inspired by a Sichuan dish called "saliva chicken," because it's so delicious it makes your mouth water. In Japanese, we've translated it as yodare dori. I like adding fresh vegetables and eating it as a salad in the summer. The spiciness of the sauce whets your appetite on those hot days when you don't feel all that hungry. This is a great make-ahead salad, as both the chicken and the sauce can be prepared in advance, and you'll just need to assemble everything right before serving. Feel free to adjust the amount of crushed red pepper based on your heat preference. For salads, I like to soak the raw onion in cold water to remove some of its bite.

Serves 4

CHICKEN

4 chicken tenders (about 8 ounces total)

Kosher salt and freshly ground black pepper

2 tablespoons sake

2 (¼-inch-thick) slices fresh ginger

SAUCE

¼ cup soy sauce

3 tablespoons rice vinegar

2 tablespoons toasted sesame oil

1 tablespoon sugar

1 teaspoon miso

1 teaspoon finely grated garlic

1 teaspoon finely grated fresh ginger

2 tablespoons toasted white sesame seeds

1 teaspoon crushed red pepper flakes

SALAD

½ red onion

1 cucumber, cut into thin matchsticks

1 tomato, cut into wedges

1 bunch cilantro, leaves picked

1. MAKE THE CHICKEN: Remove the tendon (white string) from the chicken tenders by using a fork to secure one end of the tendon, then with a paper towel or tweezers, pull on the tendon to remove it. Season the chicken with salt and pepper.

2. In a medium skillet, combine the sake, ginger, and 2 tablespoons water. Add the chicken and bring to a simmer over medium-high heat. Reduce the heat to low, cover, and cook until the chicken is cooked through, about 5 minutes. Remove the skillet from the heat and let cool to room temperature, covered, 30 minutes to 1 hour.

3. Shred the chicken into about ½-inch-thick pieces. The chicken will keep in an airtight container in the refrigerator for up to 3 days.

4. MAKE THE SAUCE: In a small bowl, combine the soy sauce, rice vinegar, sesame oil, sugar, miso, garlic, ginger, sesame seeds, and pepper flakes. Stir well until the sugar and miso are dissolved. The sauce will keep in an airtight container in the refrigerator for up to 3 days.

5. MAKE THE SALAD: Fill a medium bowl with cold water. Thinly slice the onion and add it to the water. Soak for 10 minutes. Drain and pat dry.

6. In a large bowl, toss the chicken, cucumber, tomato, onion, and cilantro. Drizzle with the sauce and serve immediately.

Curry Rice

カレーライス

Known as karē raisu in Japanese, curry rice is one of the first recipes I ever learned to cook. When I was in elementary school, we went camping every summer with other children in the neighborhood. Curry rice was one of our staple meals on this trip, and all the students would participate in preparing it in giant pots over the campfire.

The most common way of making Japanese curry is using premade curry roux (カレールー), which you can buy at all grocery stores in Japan. It comes in cubes that easily dissolve into a thick sauce to serve over rice. The texture of Japanese curry is more like gravy, and it has a milder flavor than South and Southeast Asian curries. It's a comforting dish I'll make when I don't feel like cooking or have run out of ideas for dinner. I've always used boxed curry roux and never thought to make it myself. When I worked as a restaurant line cook, however, my co-worker and friend Luke made it from scratch for our family meals. I was so impressed—it was more delicious than the store-bought curry roux and didn't contain unwanted additives such as refined palm oil.

Serves 4

CURRY ROUX

2 tablespoons S&B curry powder

1 teaspoon ground coriander

1 teaspoon ground cumin

4 tablespoons (½ stick) unsalted butter

¼ cup all-purpose flour

1 tablespoon cornstarch

1 tablespoon honey

CHICKEN CURRY

1 tablespoon neutral oil, such as canola or grapeseed

1 pound boneless, skinless chicken thighs, cut into 1½-inch pieces

1 yellow onion, cut into ½-inch slices (about 2½ cups)

1 tablespoon finely grated fresh ginger

2 garlic cloves, finely grated

2 Yukon Gold potatoes, peeled and cut into 1½-inch pieces (about 2 cups)

2 carrots, cut into 1-inch pieces (about 1½ cups)

1 quart low-sodium chicken broth

1 bay leaf

2 teaspoons kosher salt, plus more to taste

1 teaspoon Worcestershire sauce

¼ cup peeled and grated Fuji apple (about ½ apple)

Freshly cooked rice (see page 115), for serving

tips | I tested several brands of curry powders and found that Japanese S&B curry powder lends the familiar flavor that I wanted. You can find it at Japanese grocery stores or online.

• The spice level for this curry is mild. If you like heat, add cayenne pepper to taste.

(recipe continues)

1. MAKE THE CURRY ROUX: In a medium skillet, combine the curry powder, coriander, and cumin. Cook over medium heat, stirring, until fragrant, about 3 minutes. Transfer to a small bowl.

2. Line a small baking dish or heatproof container with parchment paper. (I like to use a 4-inch square Pyrex dish.) In the same medium skillet, melt the butter over medium heat. Sprinkle with the flour and cornstarch and cook, stirring constantly, until pale brown, about 8 minutes. At first, the texture will be similar to wet sand. When the flour is cooked through, it will have a smoother texture. Add the toasted spice mixture and stir to combine. Add the honey and stir to combine. Transfer the mixture to the prepared container and let cool to room temperature. Refrigerate until ready to use. To store the curry roux, cut into 2-inch cubes. It will keep in an airtight container in the refrigerator for up to 2 weeks, or in the freezer for up to 2 months.

3. MAKE THE CHICKEN CURRY: In a Dutch oven or large heavy pot, heat the oil over medium-high heat. Add the chicken and cook until lightly browned and cooked through, about 3 minutes per side. Transfer the chicken to a plate.

4. To the pot, add the onion and cook, stirring, until soft, about 4 minutes. Add the ginger and garlic and cook, stirring, until fragrant, about 2 minutes. Add the potatoes and carrots. Cook, stirring, until the vegetables are coated with oil, 2 to 3 minutes. Return the chicken to the pot.

5. Add the chicken broth and bring to a boil. Reduce the heat to medium and add the bay leaf. Bring to a simmer and cook, stirring occasionally, until the potatoes and carrots are tender, 15 to 20 minutes.

6. Transfer about ½ cup of cooking liquid to a bowl. Break the curry roux into smaller pieces. Add half of the curry roux to the cooking liquid and stir to dissolve. Add the curry mixture to the pot. Repeat with another ½ cup of cooking liquid and the remaining curry roux. Add the curry mixture to the pot and stir to combine.

7. Add the salt, Worcestershire sauce, and grated apple. Cook until thickened, about 10 minutes. Taste and season with more salt, if desired. The curry will be quite thick. If you prefer a thinner curry, add a splash of water. Serve with the rice.

Rib-Eye Steak
with Shoyu-Garlic Sauce

ガーリック醤油ステーキ

I started cooking more steak when I moved to the States because you rarely see thick cuts of meat in grocery stores in Japan. One of my favorite ways to serve steak is on a bed of white rice, since the rice soaks up the juices and becomes so incredibly flavorful. This is my husband's favorite dish, so I'll often make it for special occasions such as his birthday or our anniversary. It's also perfect for a small celebration or dinner party, since you can splurge on a nice piece of meat and serve it family-style. It's quite impressive when presented on a platter with the arugula-radish salad scattered around the steak. There's a double dose of garlic for additional flavor—cooked into the butter-soy sauce and fried into garlic chips for a crunchy topping.

Serves 4

GARLIC CHIPS

3 tablespoons neutral oil, such as canola or grapeseed

3 garlic cloves, thinly sliced

STEAK

1 pound boneless rib-eye steak, about 1½ inches thick

Kosher salt

SOY-GARLIC SAUCE

1 tablespoon unsalted butter

1 garlic clove, finely grated

2 tablespoons mirin

2 tablespoons soy sauce

ARUGULA SALAD

1 cup lightly packed baby arugula

½ fennel bulb, thinly sliced (about ½ cup)

2 radishes, thinly sliced

1 tablespoon extra-virgin olive oil

Juice of ¼ lemon (about 1 tablespoon)

Kosher salt and freshly ground black pepper

RICE

3 cups freshly cooked rice (see page 115)

2 tablespoons finely chopped fresh parsley leaves

1. MAKE THE GARLIC CHIPS: Line a plate with paper towels. In a small skillet, heat the neutral oil over medium heat. Add the garlic and cook until golden brown, about 5 minutes. Using a slotted spoon or fork, transfer the garlic to the paper towels to drain. Set aside. Reserve 2 tablespoons of the garlic oil for the steak.

2. MAKE THE STEAK: Generously season the steak on both sides with salt. Let sit at room temperature for 30 minutes. Pat the steak dry with paper towels.

3. In a cast-iron pan or large skillet, heat the reserved 2 tablespoons garlic oil over high heat. Add the steak and cook until medium-rare, about 5 minutes per side. (For rare, cook about 4 minutes per side.) Transfer the steak to a cutting board and let rest for 10 minutes.

(recipe continues)

4. MEANWHILE, MAKE THE SOY-GARLIC SAUCE: In a small skillet, melt the butter over medium heat. Add the garlic and cook until fragrant, about 1 minute. Add the mirin and simmer for 15 seconds to evaporate some of the alcohol. Add the soy sauce and remove the skillet from the heat.

5. MAKE THE ARUGULA SALAD: In a large bowl, combine the arugula, fennel, and radishes. Drizzle with the olive oil and lemon juice and toss to combine. Season with salt and pepper.

6. MAKE THE RICE AND SERVE: In a large bowl, combine the rice and parsley and mix well. Transfer the rice to a large platter or serving plate. Slice the steak against the grain and place it over the rice. Drizzle with the sauce and top with the garlic chips. Scatter the arugula salad around the steak.

tip | Use a metal cake tester to check the doneness of the steak. Insert the tester all the way into the steak on a diagonal and wait for 3 seconds. Press the tester against your lip or wrist. If the tester is cold in the middle, the steak is rare. If it's slightly warm, almost like the temperature of your skin, it's medium-rare. You can also use a meat thermometer: 115°F for rare and 125°F for medium rare.

Ginger Pork Chops

ポークチョップのしょうが焼き

Ginger pork, or buta no shogayaki in Japanese, is a very popular dish in Japan, and is usually made with thinly sliced pork, which can be found presliced in Japanese grocery stores. When I moved to the US, I started using pork chops and adjusted the cooking method for the thicker cut. With thin slices, you don't need to season the meat with salt and pepper because the sauce is so flavorful on its own, and the pork and sauce cook together in the skillet. But with a thicker pork chop, it's important to season both sides with salt and pepper and cook the sauce separately from the pork. The skillet needs to be very hot for searing the pork chops, but it will be too hot for the ginger-soy sauce, which contains sugar and would burn if added at the same time as the pork. I love serving this dish with the Cabbage Salad with Lemon-Miso Dressing (page 54) and a bowl of white rice. Put a piece of pork onto the rice and allow the sauce to soak into the grains, then alternate with bites of refreshing cabbage.

Serves 4

2 bone-in pork chops (1½ to 2 pounds total), 1 inch thick

Kosher salt and freshly ground black pepper

¼ cup soy sauce

2 tablespoons mirin

1 tablespoon sake

½ teaspoon sugar

1 tablespoon finely grated fresh ginger

2 tablespoons neutral oil, such as canola or grapeseed

1. Season the pork chops with salt and pepper on both sides.

2. In a small bowl, combine the soy sauce, mirin, sake, sugar, and ginger. Whisk to combine and set aside.

3. In a large skillet, heat the oil over high heat. Add the pork chops and cook until golden brown and cooked through, 5 to 7 minutes per side. Transfer the pork chops to a plate and let rest for 5 to 10 minutes.

4. In a small skillet, bring the ginger-soy mixture to a boil over medium-high heat and simmer for 1 minute. Take care not to simmer it for too long, or it will turn into a thick glaze. You just want to evaporate the alcohol from the mirin and sake and remove the sharp flavor of raw ginger.

5. Slice the pork chops off the bone, then cut them against the grain into ½-inch slices. Drizzle with the ginger-soy sauce.

Chā Shū

チャーシュー

Chā shū—braised pork belly—is a popular topping for ramen and one of my favorites. Although this recipe takes a while (the pork belly needs to marinate overnight, ideally), don't be discouraged as each step is quite easy and I promise it's worth your time. This way you can have restaurant-quality pork belly at home. You can eat it as a side dish or simply over a bowl of white rice. If it's served as a side, I would accompany it with the Potato Salad (page 50) or a simple salad.

Makes about 30 slices

PORK BELLY

1½ pounds skinless pork belly (about 6 × 8 inches)

2 tablespoons sake

2 garlic cloves, smashed

2 (¼-inch-thick) slices fresh ginger

2 scallions, cut into 4-inch pieces

1 tablespoon neutral oil, such as canola or grapeseed

MARINADE

¼ cup plus 2 tablespoons soy sauce

2 tablespoons sake

2 tablespoons honey

1 garlic clove, smashed

1 (¼-inch-thick) slice fresh ginger

1 star anise

4 Soft-Boiled Eggs (optional; page 151), peeled

1. MAKE THE PORK BELLY: Using a fork, prick the surface of both sides of the pork belly. Using a sharp knife, score long lines, about ¼ inch deep and 1 inch apart, on the flesh side (not the fatty side). This will make it easier to roll. Tightly roll the pork belly, fat side out, like a jelly roll. Make sure there are no gaps between the layers. Cut 3 pieces of butcher's twine and tie the pork belly very tightly, 1 to 1½ inches apart.

2. Place the pork belly in a large pot. Make a parchment cartouche (see page 23) to fit inside the pot and set aside. Add the sake, garlic, ginger, and scallions. Add enough water to cover the pork belly. Bring to a boil over high heat, using a spoon or a mesh skimmer to skim off any impurities that rise to the surface. Reduce the heat to low and bring to a simmer. Add the cartouche and cover with a lid. Cook until a fork can be easily inserted into the center of the pork, about 1½ hours.

3. Using tongs, discard the cartouche and carefully transfer the pork to a plate. Strain the cooking liquid through a fine-mesh sieve and discard the solids. Reserve 1 cup of the cooking liquid.

4. In a large nonstick skillet, heat the oil over medium-high heat. Add the pork belly and cook until golden brown on all sides, about 8 minutes. Transfer the pork to a medium pot.

5. MAKE THE MARINADE: Add the reserved cooking liquid to the pork. Add the soy sauce, sake, honey, garlic, ginger, and star anise. Bring to a boil over high heat, then reduce the heat to medium-low and simmer for 10 minutes. Remove the pot from the heat and let cool to room temperature, about 30 minutes.

6. Transfer the pork and marinade to a resealable plastic bag or an airtight container. Add the soft-boiled eggs, if using. Refrigerate at least 3 hours and ideally up to overnight. Turn the pork and eggs once or twice to evenly marinate.

7. Remove the pork from the marinade and discard the strings. (Reserve the marinade.) Slice the pork into ⅛-inch-thick slices. Halve the eggs, if using.

8. Heat a nonstick skillet over medium heat. Add the sliced pork and cook until slightly golden, about 2 minutes per side. Transfer the pork slices to a plate. Add ¼ cup of the marinade to the skillet and cook until thickened, about 3 minutes.

9. Drizzle the sauce over the pork and serve with eggs (if using). The pork and marinade will keep in an airtight container in the refrigerator for up to 5 days or frozen up to 3 months.

tip | If the pork belly is uneven in thickness, pound the thicker side with a rolling pin. If the pork is too thick to roll, pound it to flatten. If it's too narrow to roll, fold it in half to make a cylinder shape.

Nikujaga

肉じゃが

Nikujaga, a Japanese-style beef and potato stew, is the ultimate comfort food for me. It's such a simple dish, but each family has its own recipe. I grew up eating mine with thinly sliced beef, one of the most popular cuts of meat in Japan. When I moved to the US, I started using ground beef as a substitute, as it's hard to find thinly sliced beef here. It cooks just as quickly and imparts the same flavor. The sweet-salty braising liquid and parchment cartouche method infuse the vegetables with flavor. Although there's beef, it's not a meat-heavy dish. I almost think of it as a potato stew. You can make a version without beef, but in that case, use dashi instead of water for a richer broth. I like to serve nikujaga as a side dish with rice and other small plates, such as Oven-Roasted Salmon (page 94) or Tonkatsu (page 87), and vegetables that are not braised in a soy-based sauce.

Serves 4

1 tablespoon toasted sesame oil

4 Yukon Gold potatoes (about 1½ pounds), peeled and cut into 2-inch pieces

1 medium carrot, cut into 1-inch pieces (about ½ cup)

1 yellow onion, cut into ½-inch slices (about 2½ cups)

½ pound ground beef

2 tablespoons sugar

¼ cup plus 1 tablespoon soy sauce

2 tablespoons sake

1 tablespoon mirin

1. Make a parchment cartouche (see page 23) that will fit inside a large pot or a Dutch oven.

2. Set the large pot or Dutch oven over medium-high heat and heat the sesame oil. Add the potatoes, carrot, and onion. Cook, stirring, until the vegetables are coated with oil, 2 to 3 minutes.

3. Add 1½ cups water and bring to a boil. Add the ground beef and stir to combine. Bring to a simmer, using a spoon or a mesh skimmer to skim off any impurities that rise to the surface. Add the sugar and cook until dissolved, 2 to 3 minutes. Add the soy sauce, sake, and mirin. Place the cartouche over the stew (no need to cover with the lid) and cook until the potatoes are tender, about 15 minutes.

4. Remove the cartouche and simmer until all the ingredients are very tender and the liquid has reduced a bit, about 15 minutes. The consistency should be between a braised dish and a stew. Serve hot or warm.

tip | It's important to skim any impurities off the stew, especially after adding the ground beef. The impurities rise to the surface while the stew cooks, and by removing them you will have a clearer broth or braising liquid. Use a mesh skimmer or a large spoon and try not to spoon too much liquid along with the solids.

tamagoyaki

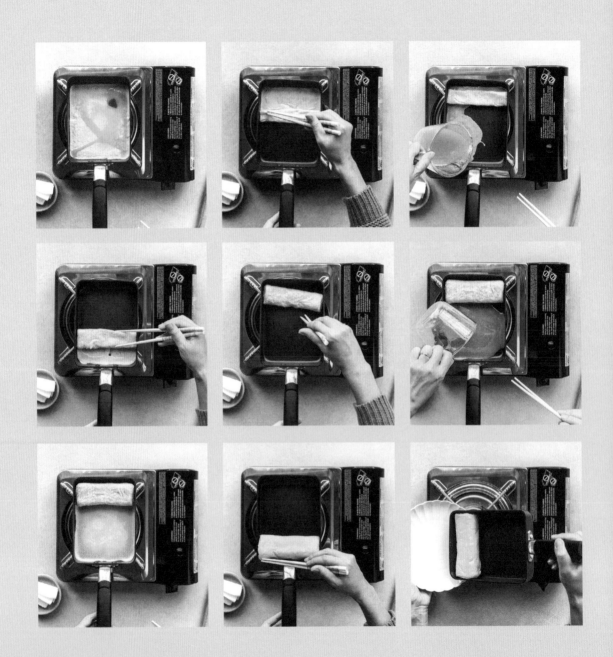

Rolled Omelet　たまご焼き

Tamagoyaki is a Japanese rolled omelet that is shaped like a rectangular log and has many layers, almost like a rolled crêpe. It's cut crosswise into thick slices and served as a side. Unlike a French omelet, the inside is cooked through and won't be runny, but the texture remains soft and light. To make the iconic log shape, you will need a special rectangular pan designed for making these omelets (see Tamagoyaki Pan, page 25). You can also make tamagoyaki in a small nonstick skillet and cut the ends to even out its shape, but the omelet will be a bit harder to roll. Tamagoyaki pans can be purchased at Japanese grocery stores or online. The traditional tamagoyaki pan is made of copper, but most modern ones are nonstick, making it easier to shape and slide the omelet.

There are so many ways of cooking tamagoyaki, but this is how my mother always made it for me, with just a little sugar and salt so it's slightly sweet. The tamagoyaki-cooking method allows for each layer of egg to cook evenly, resulting in a tender omelet. You will only need one to three slices per person as an accompaniment. My favorite slices are the end pieces, where the egg is a little crispier, much like the corner pieces of brownies.

Serves 2 to 4

3 large eggs

1 tablespoon sugar

Pinch of kosher salt

½ teaspoon neutral oil, such as canola or grapeseed

1. Crack the eggs into a spouted liquid measuring cup, a small pitcher, or a bowl. Add the sugar, salt, and 2 tablespoons water. Using chopsticks or a fork, beat the eggs until the egg whites are completely blended with the yolks. (Try not to incorporate too much air when you mix the eggs, so the egg mixture cooks evenly.) Set aside.

2. In a tamagoyaki pan or a small nonstick skillet, heat the oil over medium-high heat. Wipe out the excess oil with a paper towel. Keep the oil-soaked paper towel nearby. Check that the pan is hot by first dipping chopsticks into the egg mixture and then touching the pan; the egg should immediately set and sizzle.

3. Reduce the heat to medium. Add about ¼ cup of the egg mixture to the pan. Quickly swirl the pan to evenly spread the egg mixture. Pop any air bubbles with the tip of chopsticks. Once the egg mixture is half-set, about 30 seconds, use chopsticks to gently roll the egg from top to bottom (rolling from the far side of the pan toward you and the handle of the pan), about three rolls. Push the rolled egg to the top of the pan, away from you, to make space for more egg mixture.

4. Pour another ¼ cup of the egg mixture into the pan. Using chopsticks, lift the rolled egg, allowing the raw egg mixture to

(recipe continues)

spread beneath it. When the egg is half-set, about 30 seconds, again roll the egg from top to bottom toward you and then push the egg roll to the top of the pan, away from you. Repeat this process until all of the egg mixture is used up. Wipe the pan with the oil-soaked paper towel between rolls, if needed.

5. Transfer the rolled omelet to a cutting board and wrap with foil. Set aside until cool to the touch, about 15 minutes. The residual heat will continue to cook the egg. Remove the foil and cut the omelet into 1-inch-thick slices. The omelet will keep in an airtight container in the refrigerator for up to 2 days.

tips | If you have a spouted liquid measuring cup, use it for the eggs. It'll make it much easier to pour the eggs into the pan.

• For a chive rolled omelet, crack 3 large eggs into a liquid measuring cup, a small pitcher, or a bowl. Add 2 tablespoons finely chopped chives, 1 teaspoon sugar, 1 teaspoon soy sauce, a pinch of kosher salt, and 2 tablespoons awase or kombu dashi (store-bought or homemade, see page 32) or water. Using chopsticks or a fork, beat the eggs until the egg whites are completely blended into the yolks. Cook the tamagoyaki as directed starting at step 2.

Tonkatsu

とんかつ

My mom used pork tenderloin instead of pork loin chops when she made tonkatsu. It's more tender and makes for smaller cutlets, so they're the perfect size for a bento. The pork is usually dredged in flour, eggs, and panko. Last time I was in Japan, though, my sister taught me a hack to simplify the process: You combine two steps by making a batter with eggs, water, and flour. It's quicker, less messy, and cuts down on the dishes. This technique is quite popular in Japan for other deep-fried dishes, such as fried shrimp and croquettes.

Tonkatsu is often served with tonkatsu sauce (available at Japanese supermarkets), but I also like eating it plain without condiments. Sometimes I'll just season with a little sea salt. You can play around with other condiments, such as a squeeze of ketchup or a sprinkle of soy sauce or Worcestershire sauce, to find your favorite combination. The Lemon Miso (page 56) is delicious as a dipping sauce and provides a welcome brightness to the fried pork.

Serves 4

2 large eggs

⅓ cup all-purpose flour

2 cups panko bread crumbs

1 pound pork tenderloin

Kosher salt and freshly ground black pepper

Neutral oil, such as canola or grapeseed, for frying

Flaky sea salt, such as Maldon, for serving

Cabbage Salad with Lemon-Miso Dressing (page 54), for serving

1. In a medium bowl, combine the eggs and ¼ cup water. Using chopsticks or a fork, whisk until blended. Add the flour and mix well to combine. Set aside. Place the panko in a shallow dish and set aside.

2. Slice the pork crosswise into 1-inch-thick medallions. You should have about 8 medallions. Using the back of your knife, gently pound both sides of the pork to flatten it until it is ½ inch thick. Season both sides with kosher salt and pepper.

3. Working with one piece at a time, dip the pork into the egg-flour mixture, allowing any excess to drain off. Press the pork into the panko to coat both sides. Transfer to a plate.

4. Line a large plate with paper towels. Pour about 1 inch of oil into a large deep pot or Dutch oven. Heat the oil over medium heat until it registers 340°F on a deep-fry thermometer.

If you don't have a thermometer, add a few crumbs of panko to the oil. The oil is the right temperature when the crumbs immediately rise to the surface.

5. Working in batches, fry the pork, flipping once or twice, until cooked through and golden brown, 3 to 4 minutes. Transfer the pork cutlets to the paper towels to drain.

6. Sprinkle the pork cutlets with flaky sea salt and serve with the cabbage salad. The pork cutlets will keep in an airtight container in the refrigerator for up to 3 days.

tips | Be gentle when you pound the pork to flatten it. It's already tender, so you don't need to tenderize it.

• Use leftover pork cutlets to make Katsu Don (page 127) or Katsu Sandos (page 243).

seafood

93
Japanese Breakfast

97
Parchment-Baked
Lemon Miso Salmon

98
Salmon and Vegetable
Nanbanzuke

101
Miso Cod with Swiss Chard

102
Red Snapper Nitsuke

105
Pan-Seared Fish
with Scallion-Lemon Oil

106
Shrimp in Chili Sauce

109
Shrimp and
Mixed Vegetable Kakiage

110
Sake-Steamed Clams

japanese
breakfast

Japanese breakfast is my ultimate comfort food. It comprises several savory dishes that in combination create a balanced and filling meal. Here are the components of the typical Japanese breakfast my mom used to make when I was growing up: grilled fish (such as salmon or salted mackerel), tsukemono (pickled vegetables) or a vegetable side dish (such as potato salad or soy sauce–simmered kabocha), tamagoyaki (rolled omelet), miso soup, natto (fermented soybeans), and a bowl of rice with nori (seaweed). Although there are many small dishes in a Japanese breakfast, my mom could quickly throw the meal together without much thought and made it look so easy.

Most of the dishes can be prepared beforehand, or sometimes we'll supplement with leftovers. Unlike my mom, however, I struggle to find the time to make the full spread in the mornings. But because Japanese breakfast is still one of my favorite meals, I like to make it for lunch or even dinner. No matter the time of day, it always makes me very content.

Natto is fermented soybeans. It's a very acquired taste, in part because of its slimy texture. But the flavor itself is nutty, and I always serve it as part of a Japanese breakfast. You can find natto in Japanese grocery stores, usually in the refrigerated or frozen section. Before eating, mix the natto with chopsticks until stringy, almost like cotton candy. Often the natto comes with a packet of seasoning, which you can add, though I also like to just season with a sprinkle of soy sauce. To eat it, I wrap some natto and rice with nori and eat it like a temaki (hand roll) or a taco, as my husband says.

Here, I've included recipes for roasted salmon and quick pickles. See page 115 for Japanese white rice, pages 34 and 37 for miso soup, and page 84 for tamagoyaki. All together this will serve four for breakfast.

Other breakfast side dishes that you could add or play around with, especially if you have leftovers, include the Potato Salad (page 50), Cabbage Salad with Lemon-Miso Dressing (page 54), Green Salad with Umeboshi Dressing (page 57), Cucumber and Fennel Sunomono (page 53), and Soy Sauce–Simmered Kabocha (page 38).

Oven-Roasted Salmon 焼き鮭

A lot of Japanese stovetops come with a small grill for grilling fish. Grilled salmon is commonly served for breakfast. When I cook salmon for breakfast, I don't salt it because I drizzle soy sauce on top. I recommend wrapping some salmon, rice, and quick pickles in a piece of nori (seaweed).

4 skin-on salmon fillets (4 ounces each)

Soy sauce, for serving

1. Preheat the oven to 400°F. Line a sheet pan with parchment paper.

2. Place the salmon on the prepared pan, skin-side down. Roast until cooked through, about 20 minutes. The salmon is done when a sharp knife inserted into the thickest part releases clear juices.

3. Sprinkle with the soy sauce and serve immediately.

Quick Pickles 即席漬け

I love this quick pickling method because it's much faster than pickling with vinegar. It's perfect for when you want to add an easy vegetable side that comes together in 15 minutes. Sometimes I skip the sesame oil and add just a few drops of soy sauce.

2 Persian (mini) cucumbers, thinly sliced (about 2 cups)

1 Japanese or Chinese eggplant, halved and sliced ¼ inch thick (about 1 cup)

1 teaspoon kosher salt

1 teaspoon toasted sesame oil

1 tablespoon toasted white sesame seeds, coarsely ground (see Tip, page 41)

1. Place the cucumbers and eggplant in a medium bowl. Sprinkle with the salt and toss to combine. Set aside for 10 minutes.

2. Using your hands, squeeze out as much moisture as possible from the vegetables. Discard the liquid in the bowl and return the vegetables to the bowl. Add the sesame oil and toss to coat. Sprinkle with the ground sesame seeds. The pickles will keep in an airtight container in the refrigerator for up to 3 days.

Salt-Pickled Cabbage 白菜の即席漬け

The basic rule for making quick pickles is to use an amount of salt that is 2% of the vegetable's weight and to press the vegetables with something that is about three times as heavy as they are. I often use cans of sparkling water to weight down the cabbage.

1 pound napa cabbage

1 (4-inch) square piece kombu

1 dried árbol chile pepper

1½ teaspoons fine sea salt

Soy sauce, for serving

1. Remove the cabbage leaves from the core. Wash each leaf well, shaking off excess water. Cut the leaves crosswise into 1-inch-wide strips.

2. Using kitchen scissors, cut the kombu into thin slices that are about 2 × ⅛ inch.

3. Using kitchen scissors, cut the chile into thin rings that are about ⅛ inch wide.

4. In a large bowl, combine the cabbage and salt. Using your hands, mix well to evenly distribute the salt. Add the kombu and chile and mix well with your hands.

5. Transfer the cabbage mixture to a large resealable plastic bag. Remove the air from the bag and close tightly. Place the bag on a sheet pan or large plate and lay flat. Place another baking sheet or plate on top, then place a heavy item (it should weigh about 3 pounds, or three times the weight of the cabbage) on top. Refrigerate for at least 3 hours and up to 4 days.

6. When ready to serve, squeeze out the liquid from the cabbage. Serve with a small amount of soy sauce for dipping, or drizzle with about ½ teaspoon soy sauce. The pickled cabbage will keep in an airtight container in the refrigerator up to 4 days more.

Parchment-Baked Lemon Miso Salmon

鮭のレモン味噌包み焼き

Packed with lots of flavors, this recipe is versatile and easy. If you don't have leeks, use thinly sliced onions or shallots. No fingerling potatoes? Replace them with thinly sliced Yukon Gold. Any kind of mushroom works well, too, such as sliced shiitakes. You can also substitute the salmon with another fish fillet, such as cod, halibut, or snapper.

The salmon steams in the parchment paper and absorbs the flavors of all the accompanying ingredients. It's a foolproof method for tender fish, as the moisture is trapped inside the parchment. This "all-in-one" recipe is especially fun to make for guests. I like to serve it on individual plates so that each guest can open their packet to discover what's hidden inside.

Serves 4

12 ounces fingerling potatoes, cut crosswise into ¼-inch-thick slices (about 2¼ cups)

4 ounces oyster mushrooms, stemmed and torn into bite-size pieces (about 2 cups)

1 medium leek, white part only, thinly sliced (about ¾ cup)

4 tablespoons (½ stick) unsalted butter, thinly sliced or broken apart with your fingers

Kosher salt and freshly ground black pepper

8 tablespoons Lemon Miso (page 56)

4 skinless salmon fillets (3 ounces each)

4 tablespoons white wine or sake

1. Preheat the oven to 400°F with racks in the upper and lower thirds.

2. Cut four 12-inch square pieces of parchment paper. Position each piece of parchment with a corner facing you in a diamond shape.

3. Evenly divide the potatoes among the pieces of parchment, placing them in the center. Top with the mushrooms and leek. Scatter ½ tablespoon of the butter over each vegetable pile. Season with salt and pepper. Drizzle each with 1 tablespoon of the lemon miso.

4. Put a salmon fillet on top of each vegetable pile and season with salt and pepper. Coat each salmon fillet with 1 tablespoon lemon miso, then sprinkle with 1 tablespoon of the white wine and top with ½ tablespoon of the butter.

5. Working with one parchment piece at a time, take the corner closest to you and the one opposite. Lift the corners to meet in the middle and fold them together three or four times to seal. Twist the remaining two corners, completely sealing the fish and vegetables inside. Transfer the parchment packets to two sheet pans.

6. Bake for 20 minutes, switching racks from top to bottom halfway through. (The salmon and potatoes should be fully cooked through, but if they aren't, just close up the parchment packet again and return to the oven for a few minutes more.)

7. Serve immediately. Be careful not to burn yourself with the steam when you open the packets.

Salmon and Vegetable Nanbanzuke

鮭の南蛮漬け

This marinated fish with vegetables is one of the many dishes my mother made all the time. I would always ask her for the recipe, but since she didn't measure any of the ingredients, even for the marinade, I had to tinker with the amounts to find the right flavor. For her version, she would use yellow onions and small whole horse mackerel. The vinegar disintegrates the fish bones, so you can eat the whole fish. I swapped in red onion, yellow pepper, and salmon for a more festive look. You can use any onion or a white fish—just make sure to fry the fish first, so it holds its shape. I know you'll want to eat the dish right away, but I promise it's worth the wait and will taste much better on the second or third day. The marinade gently pickles the vegetables and salmon, and the sharp vinegar flavor mellows out over time. Because it's served cold, salmon nanbanzuke is especially good on a hot summer day.

Serves 4

1 red onion, thinly sliced (about 2 cups)

1 carrot, cut into thin matchsticks or grated (about 1 cup)

1 yellow bell pepper, thinly sliced (about 1 cup)

1 pound skinless salmon, cut into 2 × 1-inch pieces

Kosher salt and freshly ground black pepper

2 tablespoons all-purpose flour

2 tablespoons neutral oil, such as canola or grapeseed

MARINADE

1 cup rice vinegar

3 tablespoons sake

2 tablespoons mirin

1 teaspoon soy sauce

3 tablespoons sugar

1 dried red chile, sliced and seeded, or ¼ teaspoon crushed red pepper flakes

tip | Cut the vegetables as thinly as possible since you won't be cooking them.

1. In a large ceramic or glass baking dish, combine the onion, carrot, and bell pepper. Stir well and spread in an even layer. Set aside.

2. Pat the salmon dry with a paper towel. Season it all over with salt and pepper. Place the flour on a plate. Working with one piece at a time, coat the salmon in the flour and transfer it to another plate.

3. In a large nonstick skillet, heat the oil over medium-high heat. Add the salmon and cook until golden brown and cooked through, about 3 minutes per side. Arrange the salmon on top of the vegetables in an even layer.

4. MAKE THE MARINADE: In a small pot, combine the rice vinegar, sake, mirin, soy sauce, sugar, chile, and ⅔ cup water. Bring to a boil over medium heat, stirring to dissolve the sugar, about 8 minutes.

5. Immediately pour the hot marinade over the salmon and vegetables. Let cool to room temperature, 30 to 40 minutes. Flip the salmon and vegetables, covering most of the salmon with the vegetables.

6. Cover the dish with plastic wrap and refrigerate for at least 12 hours and up to 3 days. Serve cold.

tips | If the fish is on the thinner side (less than 1 inch thick), marinate for no more than 30 minutes.

• You can freeze the marinated fish: Remove the fish from the marinade and wrap the fillets individually in plastic. Place in a resealable plastic bag and freeze for up to 1 month. If the fish was previously frozen, you cannot freeze it again.

Miso Cod with Swiss Chard

鱈の味噌焼きとスイスチャードのあえもの

Sweet miso-marinated fish or meat is a traditional Japanese dish called saikyo-yaki. It's usually made with saikyo-miso, a sweeter and milder miso from Kyoto. My recipe is inspired by those flavors but uses regular miso. Make sure to remove the excess miso paste from the fish before cooking it; otherwise, it will overpower the fish. Since the miso-marinated fish is very flavorful and savory, I love to serve it with a simple vegetable side, such as the sesame oil–dressed Swiss chard here.

You may recognize this dish from Japanese restaurants in the US. It's often quite expensive there, when really it's so easy and quick to make at home. I especially like how the miso marinade melts into the soft flakes of cod, but it also works well with other fish, such as salmon and halibut. Just make sure to choose a fillet that is at least 1 inch thick.

Serves 4

MISO MARINATED FISH

2 tablespoons mirin

1 tablespoon sake

2 tablespoons light brown sugar

¼ cup miso

4 skinless or skin-on cod or sablefish fillets (5 ounces each)

SWISS CHARD

Kosher salt

2 bunches of Swiss chard (about 1¼ pounds)

2 tablespoons toasted sesame oil

1 teaspoon fresh lemon juice

1 teaspoon toasted white sesame seeds

1. MAKE THE MISO-MARINATED FISH: In a small pot, combine the mirin and sake. Bring to a boil over high heat and cook for 30 seconds to evaporate the alcohol. Remove the pot from the heat and add the brown sugar. Whisk to completely dissolve and let cool to room temperature.

2. In a small bowl, combine the mirin-sake mixture with the miso. Mix well to dissolve the miso.

3. Place the cod fillets in a shallow container. Slather the cod with the miso mixture on all sides. Cover with a lid or plastic wrap. Refrigerate for at least 30 minutes and up to overnight.

4. Preheat the oven to 450°F. Line a sheet pan with parchment paper.

5. Using a paper towel or your fingers, lightly wipe the miso paste off the cod fillets. (Don't completely wipe it off; you should still have some visible paste on the fish.) Place the cod on the prepared pan.

6. Bake until the fish is cooked through and starting to caramelize at the edges, about 10 minutes.

7. MEANWHILE, MAKE THE SWISS CHARD: Bring a large pot of salted water to a boil.

8. Remove the Swiss chard leaves from the stems. Cut the stems into ½-inch pieces. Cut the leaves into 1-inch-wide strips. Keep the stems and leaves separate.

9. Add the stems to the boiling water and cook for 1 minute. Add the leaves and cook for 1 minute more. Drain the Swiss chard and rinse under cold water. Squeeze out the excess water.

10. In a medium bowl, combine the Swiss chard, sesame oil, lemon juice, 1 teaspoon salt, and the sesame seeds. Mix well with chopsticks or tongs and serve alongside the miso-marinated cod.

Red Snapper Nitsuke

鯛の煮付け

Growing up in a small town on the Seto Inland Sea, I ate a lot of fish. Our family often received a variety of fish from relatives and family friends, so nitsuke (simmered fish) was a staple dish. Nitsuke is usually made with smaller white fish that are cooked whole, though here I've chosen red snapper fillets, which work just as nicely as the whole fish. For this recipe, I use a Japanese cooking technique called yubiki. You pour hot water over the fish fillets, or if the fillets are thick, you add the fish to boiling water and cook it just until the flesh turns white. This technique removes some of the fishy smell and helps maintain the shape of the fish while braising. I recommend serving this dish immediately while the fish is moist and soaked in the liquid. I like to accompany it with white rice or Corn Rice (page 134) and miso soup (see pages 34 and 37). The sauce is packed with flavor, so you'll want to choose mild-flavored side dishes.

Serves 4

4 skin-on red snapper fillets (5 ounces each), at room temperature (see Tip)

½ teaspoon kosher salt

Boiling water, for covering the fish (about 7 cups)

3 tablespoons sake

2 tablespoons sugar

4 thin slices fresh ginger

2 tablespoons soy sauce

1 tablespoon mirin

1. Using a sharp knife, score the fish skin by making crosshatch incisions about 1½ inches long. (This is to prevent the skin from curling when the fish cooks.) Sprinkle the salt on both sides of the fish fillets. Set aside for 10 minutes. Pat dry with a paper towel and place in a large heatproof bowl.

2. Pour in enough boiling water to cover the fish by 1 inch. Set aside until the fish turns white, about 1 minute. Discard the water. If the fish was at room temperature, it shouldn't curl too much.

3. Transfer the fish to a large pot, skin-side up. The fillets should be in a single layer, not overlapping. Once you have chosen the pot, make a parchment cartouche (see page 23) to fit inside the pot and set aside.

4. To the fish, add 1 cup water, the sake, sugar, and ginger. Bring to a boil over high heat. Reduce the heat to medium and cook for 3 minutes. Using a spoon or a mesh skimmer, skim off any impurities that rise to the surface.

5. Add the soy sauce and place the parchment cartouche on top. Cook for 10 minutes. Remove the cartouche, add the mirin, and cook until the braising liquid is reduced by about a half to one-third, about 5 minutes. Serve immediately.

tips | You could also make this dish with flounder, black cod, rockfish, sea bass, or fluke. Just make sure to keep the skin on.

• To bring fish to room temperature, let it sit on the counter for 30 minutes.

Pan-Seared Fish
with Scallion-Lemon Oil

白身魚のソテーとねぎレモンソース

One of my favorite ways to cook fish on a weeknight is on the stove. I save this dish for those especially busy days because it comes together in under 30 minutes. I like to use a firm fish, such as branzino or red snapper, which is less likely to fall apart than cod or other flaky fish. The method here is incredibly simple, just make sure to use a well-seasoned pan or a nonstick skillet and begin cooking the fish with its skin pressed down on the skillet. The scallion-lemon oil pairs well with anything, so you can also serve it with other dishes, such as roasted chicken. To keep the meal light but satisfying, accompany the pan-seared fish with a salad, such as Green Salad with Umeboshi Dressing (page 57), Cucumber and Fennel Sunomono (page 53), Potato Salad (page 50), or Loaded Vegetable Miso Soup (page 34) in the winter.

Serves 4

8 tablespoons extra-virgin olive oil

4 scallions, thinly sliced

2 garlic cloves, finely chopped

1 teaspoon finely chopped fresh ginger

2 tablespoons chopped lemon, including peel and pith (about 2 slices)

Kosher salt and freshly ground black pepper

2 teaspoons soy sauce

4 skin-on white fish fillets (6 ounces each), such as branzino, red snapper, or sea bass

3 tablespoons all-purpose flour

¼ cup coarsely chopped fresh parsley leaves

1. In a small skillet, combine 6 tablespoons of the oil, the scallions, garlic, ginger, lemon, and 1 teaspoon salt. Cook over low heat, stirring, until fragrant and the scallions are wilted, about 5 minutes. The garlic shouldn't take on any color. Remove the skillet from the heat and add the soy sauce. Set aside.

2. Pat the fish fillets dry with a paper towel. Using a sharp knife, score the fish skin by making crosswise incisions about 1½ inches long. (This is to prevent the skin from curling when the fish cooks.) Season both sides of the fish with salt and pepper. Sprinkle the flour all over the fish and shake off any excess.

3. In a large nonstick skillet, heat the remaining 2 tablespoons oil over medium-high heat. Once the oil is hot (a sprinkle of flour should immediately sizzle), add the fish fillets skin-side down. Gently press on the fish with a flexible spatula. Cook until the skin is golden brown and the flesh is opaque, about 5 minutes. (The cooking time will vary depending on the thickness of the fillets.) Flip and cook until just cooked through, about 1 minute.

4. Transfer the fish to a serving platter and spoon the scallion-lemon oil over the fish. Sprinkle with the parsley and serve immediately.

tip | Cook the fish skin-side down until almost fully cooked through. When you flip the fish, you just want it to "kiss" the pan, meaning it will briefly cook on the other side.

Shrimp in Chili Sauce

えびチリ

There is a style of Japanese-Chinese cooking called chūka. It is heavily influenced by Chinese cuisine but adapted for a Japanese palate and uses ingredients that are easily available in Japan. Examples of this style include ramen, fried rice, and Spicy Chicken Salad (page 70). Shrimp in chili sauce, or ebi chili in Japanese, is one of my favorite chūka dishes. It's usually cooked with doubanjiang, a Chinese chili paste. One day when I was craving ebi chili, I couldn't find doubanjiang at my closest grocery store. Instead, I used sriracha and it made a surprisingly delicious sauce.

You'll often find ketchup in Japanese home-cooking recipes, such as omurice (rice with omelet, page 130). It's a secret flavor booster, and sometimes we even add it to curry for a bit of sweetness. I want to encourage you to use ketchup here. It creates a sweet-savory sauce that reminds me of shrimp cocktail, but with more heat. You can serve the ebi chili with white rice.

Serves 4

CHILI SAUCE

½ cup chicken broth or water

¼ cup ketchup

1 tablespoon sriracha

1 teaspoon sake

1 teaspoon mirin

1 teaspoon toasted sesame oil

SHRIMP

3 tablespoons potato starch or cornstarch

1 pound jumbo (21/25) shrimp, peeled and deveined

Kosher salt and freshly ground black pepper

4 tablespoons plus 2 teaspoons neutral oil, such as canola or grapeseed

1 garlic clove, finely chopped

1 teaspoon finely chopped fresh ginger

1 tablespoon chopped fresh chives (optional)

tip | Shrimp cooks very quickly. It's done once the flesh turns completely opaque and pink, and the tail turns bright red.

1. MAKE THE CHILI SAUCE: In a small bowl, whisk the chicken broth, ketchup, sriracha, sake, mirin, and sesame oil. Set aside.

2. COOK THE SHRIMP: Place the potato starch on a plate. Using paper towels, pat the shrimp dry and season them with salt and pepper. Working one at a time, coat the shrimp in the potato starch. Shake off any excess starch and transfer to a plate. Set aside.

3. In a nonstick skillet, heat 2 tablespoons of the oil over medium-high heat. Add half of the shrimp and cook until pink, 1 to 2 minutes. Flip the shrimp and cook until pink and opaque, about 1 minute more. Transfer to a plate. Repeat with 2 tablespoons of the oil and the remaining shrimp.

4. Wipe the skillet with paper towels. Add the remaining 2 teaspoons oil to the skillet over medium heat. Add the garlic and ginger and cook until fragrant, about 1 minute. Add the chili sauce and bring to a simmer. Add the shrimp and stir to coat in the sauce. Don't worry if the sauce looks loose at first; the potato starch from the shrimp will thicken it. Transfer to a serving plate and garnish with the chives, if desired.

Shrimp and Mixed Vegetable Kakiage

えびと野菜のかきあげ

This easy home-style tempura, called kakiage, is a great way to use up leftover vegetables. You could swap in just about any vegetable, such as carrots, sweet potato, kabocha, asparagus, scallions, and red onion. Make sure to cut them into thin matchsticks that are all about the same size to ensure even cooking. I would avoid vegetables with a high water content, such as zucchini and eggplant, as they could make the kakiage soggy. For a main dish, serve the kakiage alongside rice and miso soup (pages 34 and 37), or with Nikujaga (page 82) for a more filling meal. You can also make smaller-size kakiage for topping udon noodles or to pack in a bento box (see page 145).

Makes about 10 pieces (serves 4)

TEMPURA BATTER

3 tablespoons all-purpose flour

3 tablespoons potato starch or cornstarch

½ teaspoon kosher salt

1 large egg

6 tablespoons ice water (see Tip, page 44)

FILLING

1 pound jumbo (21/25) shrimp, peeled and deveined, cut into ½-inch pieces

1 large Yukon Gold potato, peeled and cut into matchsticks ⅛ inch thick (about 1¼ cups)

½ yellow onion, thinly sliced (about 1 cup)

⅓ cup frozen shelled edamame, thawed

Neutral oil, such as canola or grapeseed, for frying

Flaky sea salt, such as Maldon, for sprinkling

1. MAKE THE TEMPURA BATTER: Sift the flour and potato starch into a small bowl. Stir in the kosher salt and set in the refrigerator. In another small bowl, whisk the egg and ice water. Set aside in the refrigerator.

2. MAKE THE FILLING: In a large bowl, combine the shrimp, potato, onion, and edamame. Sprinkle 2 tablespoons of the flour mixture over the vegetables and shrimp. Using chopsticks or a fork, gently toss to evenly coat. Sprinkle with the remaining flour mixture and pour the egg mixture over the vegetables and shrimp. Toss to coat with the batter, being careful not to overmix.

3. Line a sheet pan with paper towels and top with a wire rack. Pour about 1 inch of oil into a large deep pot or Dutch oven. Heat the oil over medium-high heat until it registers 350°F on a deep-fry thermometer.

4. Working in batches, use a large spoon to scoop up about ½ cup of the vegetable-shrimp mixture and gently drop it into the oil. (Use a second spoon or chopsticks to push the mixture into the oil.) Fry until golden, 2 to 4 minutes. Flip and cook on the other side until golden brown, 2 to 4 minutes more. Transfer to the wire rack and repeat with the remaining batter.

5. Sprinkle with sea salt and serve while hot.

Sake-Steamed Clams

あさりの酒蒸し

At home, we ate a lot of seafood as we lived so close to the sea. My father would go night fishing for squid, and my aunt would bring fresh mantis shrimp to our house. One of my favorite activities was clam digging with my parents and siblings. I especially loved eating clams because it was satisfying to see the empty shells pile up at the end of a meal.

Clams cook quickly, making them perfect for a weekday evening. Make sure to discard any open clams or clams with broken or cracked shells before cooking, as those are no longer alive and shouldn't be eaten. In this recipe, clams form the base for a briny broth that is finished with butter. I like to use an empty clamshell to sip the broth, or you can soak it up with thick slices of toasted bread, enjoying every last drop.

Serves 4

2 pounds Manila clams, butter clams, or littleneck clams

Kosher salt

2 tablespoons unsalted butter

1 large shallot, thinly sliced (about ⅓ cup)

4 garlic cloves, thinly sliced

¼ cup sake

½ cup awase or kombu dashi, instant or homemade (see page 32)

1 tablespoon chopped fresh chives

1. Discard any open or cracked clams. (If the clam is open, tap on the shell, and if it doesn't close, discard it.) In a large bowl, combine 3 cups cold water and 2 tablespoons salt. Stir to dissolve the salt and add the clams. There should be enough water to cover the clams. Loosely cover the bowl with foil or newspaper. (This creates a habitat similar to being under the sand.) Soak the clams for at least 30 minutes and up to 12 hours at room temperature, or in the refrigerator if it's hot in your kitchen. Discard the soaking water. Under running water, rub the clams together to remove any dirt from their shells. Drain the clams and set aside.

2. Choose a skillet or a shallow pot with a lid that is wide enough to fit the clams in a single layer. In the skillet or pot, melt 1 tablespoon of the butter over medium-high heat. Add the shallot and cook, stirring, until fragrant and softened, 1 to 2 minutes. Add the garlic and cook, stirring, until fragrant,

1 to 2 minutes. Be careful not to brown the shallots and garlic; reduce the heat if necessary.

3. Add the sake and simmer for 2 minutes to evaporate the alcohol. Add the dashi, clams, and 1 teaspoon salt, and stir to combine. Arrange the clams in a single layer and cover. Bring to a boil, then reduce the heat to medium. Simmer, covered, shaking the pan occasionally, until all the clams have opened, 3 to 8 minutes. (Start checking if the clams are opening at the 2-minute mark.) Remove the pan from the heat.

4. Cut the remaining 1 tablespoon butter into small pieces and add to the broth. Allow the butter to melt completely. Stir gently and taste the broth. Season with more salt, if desired. Transfer to a large serving bowl, sprinkle with the chives, and serve immediately.

tips | Soaking clams in salted water (very salty, like the ocean) allows them to breathe out impurities and sand.

• Be careful not to overcook the clams, or the meat will turn very rubbery. Once a few shells start to open, shake the pot a few times and start checking every minute.

rice

how to cook rice

Rice is an integral part of our daily meals in Japan. We take cooking rice very seriously. You can find many different varieties of Japanese rice and rice cookers—there's even a rice cooker that costs more than $1,000! In this section, I'll teach you how to cook the perfect bowl of Japanese rice.

Choosing Rice: Short-Grain Versus Medium-Grain

There are many kinds of Japanese rice available in the US. Often, Japanese white rice is labeled "sushi rice," but it's important to check whether the rice is medium-grain or short-grain. Short-grain rice is smaller, shinier, and a little stickier when cooked. It's the rice I recommend for making sushi or onigiri (rice balls), as it's easier to shape since the grains stick together. It's an excellent everyday rice and is my preferred rice all around. You can find it at most grocery stores—just read the packaging and make sure it says "short-grain rice." Asian supermarkets will sell large bags of rice for a much lower price. The other kind of rice you might come across is Calrose rice, such as from the brands Nishiki, Kokuho, and Botan. This is a medium-grain rice. It's a bit drier than short-grain, making it harder to shape sushi and onigiri, but can be used as a substitute for short-grain, and is a wonderful everyday rice. For the recipes in this book, I would avoid long-grain rice such as jasmine.

I usually buy a large bag of white rice and store it in an airtight container in a dry, dark place. You can find rice storage containers (kome bitsu in Japanese) at Japanese grocery stores or online. Because I eat rice every day, a bag of rice rarely lasts for more than a month in my household. If you don't eat rice that often, buy a smaller bag so it remains fresh. Stored correctly, uncooked white rice should keep for up to one year, but make sure to check the expiration date.

Measuring Rice

RICE COOKER: Most Japanese rice cookers come with a measuring cup. It's a bit smaller than a US measuring cup: 1 Japanese rice cooker cup = ¾ US cup (or 150g rice). The inner pot of the cooker has marked lines to indicate water levels, so you know how much water to add. If you are cooking 1 Japanese rice cooker cup, add water to level 1 of the inner pot. In this cookbook, all rice measurements are in US cups.

STOVETOP: For the stovetop, the rice and water ratio is 1:1. So if you are cooking 1 cup of rice, add 1 cup of water. There is also an "Asian mom" way of measuring water: Add the washed and drained rice to the pot, then place your index finger inside the pot and touch the top of the rice. Pour water to your finger's first knuckle joint. This method is convenient when you don't have a measuring cup.

Washing Rice

These days, it isn't necessary to wash rice too thoroughly because the rice milling process has greatly improved, so store-bought rice is fairly clean and has fewer brans that need to be washed off. I usually wash my rice two or three times. The water doesn't need to be completely clear, but should be slightly opaque, so you can see the rice. Rice is a dried grain and will absorb water the most when it first touches water. So even when washing rice, I recommend using filtered water, which has the cleanest taste and won't impart any unwanted flavors to the rice.

To wash rice, first add the rice to a large bowl and add enough filtered water to cover the rice. Make a claw shape with your fingers and gently swish your hand around in the rice, almost like washing your hair, being careful not to break the rice grains. Discard the water and repeat until the water is slightly opaque, two to three times total. Drain the rice in a fine-mesh sieve.

Soaking Rice

The next step after washing and draining the rice is to soak it in water. Again, I suggest using filtered water for soaking (as well as cooking) the rice, as the grains will absorb water. Add the correct amount of water for cooking the rice and soak at least 30 minutes in the summer and 1 hour in the winter. (Colder temperatures slow down the speed at which rice absorbs water.) Do not soak the rice for more than 2 hours. Many rice cookers include soaking in their cooking time, so you can probably skip this step for the rice cooker. Just follow the rice cooker's directions.

Cooking Vessels

For cooking 1½ cups rice on the stove, I recommend using a deep pot with a tight-fitting lid and no steamer hole. A small or medium Dutch oven, or a heavy pot with a lid, will work well. If the pot is too shallow or the lid too light, the water will boil over. I recommend a pot that is at least 2 quarts in capacity and 5 inches tall.

Serving Rice

In Japan, each family member has their own rice bowl (ochawan in Japanese), which is exclusively used for rice. I remember my father's rice bowl being the biggest one at the table, and how my rice bowl got bigger as I grew older. If you are looking for individual rice bowls, I recommend Korin (store in NYC and online), Toiro (store in LA and online), Utsuwa-no-Yakata (store in LA and online), and Miyake Ceramics (ships internationally). Some Japanese grocery stores also sell tableware. When you serve rice, wet the rice paddle before scooping out the rice. Cooked Japanese rice is very sticky and wetting the rice paddle prevents the rice from sticking to it. You can use a large spoon or a wooden spatula if you don't have a rice paddle.

Japanese food is usually quite flavorful or salty because you're supposed to eat it with rice. In a way, the rice is the centerpiece and the other dishes are accompaniments, meant to be eaten alongside the rice. You're alternating bites of rice with other dishes, along with sips of miso soup. The rice is usually on the left, the soup on the right, and the main dish is above the rice. The rice bowl should be placed quite close to you, so you can easily eat from it.

Storing Cooked Rice

My preferred way of storing rice is freezing it, unless I'm planning on eating it the next day. Let the rice cool to room temperature and divide it into individual portions (I do about 1 cup per portion). Tightly wrap each portion in plastic and put in a resealable plastic freezer bag. The rice can be frozen for up to 1 month. To reheat frozen rice, microwave the rice (still wrapped) for 30 seconds, then remove the plastic wrap and transfer the rice to a bowl. Cover the bowl with the same plastic wrap and microwave in 1-minute increments, mixing with a rice paddle or wooden spatula, until the rice is hot, about 2 minutes. You can also refrigerate leftover rice overnight to make fried rice the next day.

Rice (Stovetop Method) ご飯

The following recipe calls for US cup measurements, not the smaller rice-cooker cup that comes with some electric rice cookers.

Makes about 4 cups (serves 4)

1½ cups filtered water, plus more for washing rice

1½ cups short-grain or medium-grain rice

1. Wash the rice with filtered water (see Washing Rice, page 116) and drain.

2. In a small or medium Dutch oven or heavy pot with a tight-fitting lid (for more information, see Cooking Vessels, page 117), combine the 1½ cups filtered water and the washed rice. Soak for at least 30 minutes (in the summer) or 1 hour (in the winter).

3. Cover the pot and bring to a boil over medium-high heat. (You can quickly open the lid to check that the water is boiling.) Reduce the heat to low and cook until the water has been completely absorbed, about 15 minutes. If this is your first time, open the lid just long enough to check the rice. The cooking time will vary depending on the heat of your stove. If you still see bubbling water, continue to cook over low heat and check every 2 minutes. After you open the lid to check, close the lid and increase the heat to medium for 10 to 15 seconds. Steam escapes when you open the lid and the temperature inside the pot decreases, so you want to "reheat" the rice. Make note of how long it takes the rice to cook, and next time cook it for that amount of time. For example, if it takes an additional 2 minutes, next time set a timer for 17 minutes.

4. Remove the pot from the heat and keep the rice covered for 10 minutes. The rice is steaming. There's an old Japanese rule that says, "Once you start cooking rice, never remove the lid." I recommend following this rule once you're familiar with your stove and the cooking time. Ideally, you should never open the lid between cooking and steaming so that all the heat remains trapped inside the pot, and the rice finishes cooking.

5. When ready to serve, wet a rice paddle or wooden spatula, and stir the rice. The rice on top is a bit drier than the rice on the bottom, so it's important to mix the rice for a consistent texture.

Sushi Rice 酢飯

Sushi rice is flavored with rice vinegar, which has a mellower taste than white wine vinegar. For this recipe, I like to use Mizkan or Marukan rice vinegar. I don't recommend using store-bought "sushi vinegar," as it's already seasoned and tends to be too sweet. If you make your own sushi vinegar, you can adjust the sweetness to your liking. It's important to use freshly cooked rice, which better absorbs the sushi vinegar.

Makes 4 cups (serves 4)

SUSHI RICE VINEGAR

¼ cup rice vinegar

1 tablespoon sugar

1 teaspoon kosher salt

4 cups freshly cooked short-grain rice (see page 115)

1. Make the sushi rice vinegar: In a small bowl, combine the rice vinegar, sugar, and salt. Stir to dissolve the sugar and salt.

2. Place the freshly cooked short-grain rice in a large wide bowl. Using a spoon or a liquid measuring cup, drizzle a bit of sushi rice vinegar over the rice. Using a rice paddle or wooden spatula, gently mix the rice by holding the rice paddle vertical to the rice and mixing in a cutting motion to avoid smashing the rice grains. Continue drizzling the sushi rice vinegar over the rice in small quantities, mixing as you go to evenly distribute. The finished sushi rice will look shiny.

3. Fan the sushi rice to cool it down. In Japan, we use a traditional fan called uchiwa, but you can use any sturdy piece of paper, such as a magazine or piece of cardboard. Mix the rice with the rice paddle while fanning it so it evenly cools. The rice should be around the temperature of your skin.

4. Cover with plastic wrap or a damp towel until ready to use. Keep at room temperature. Do not place the sushi rice in the fridge as it will harden from the cold.

Oyako Don

親子丼

Oyako don—chicken and egg gently simmered in a richly flavored dashi, served in a bowl over steaming rice—is one of the easiest weeknight meals that's also incredibly filling. I made it all the time as a college student because it was fast and inexpensive. In Japan, we have special pans for making a single serving of oyako don. The pan has a vertical handle that allows you to easily slide the chicken and egg mixture directly over the rice. Now that I'm no longer only cooking for myself, I wanted to adapt the recipe for a larger serving that comes together entirely in one pot and can be served family-style. At home, I use a donabe (Japanese clay pot), but you can use any medium skillet or shallow pot with a lid.

Serves 4

1 large boneless, skinless chicken breast (about 8 ounces)

6 large eggs

⅔ cup awase or kombu dashi, instant or homemade (see page 32)

3 tablespoons mirin

3 tablespoons soy sauce

1 small yellow onion, thinly sliced (about 1½ cups)

1 scallion, thinly sliced

4 cups freshly cooked rice (see page 115)

1. Cut the chicken using the sogi giri technique (see Tip): Hold the knife against the chicken breast and at a 45-degree angle to the cutting board. Cut crosswise into ½-inch-thick slices. Cut those slices into 1-inch pieces.

2. Crack the eggs into a large measuring cup, a small pitcher, or a medium bowl. Lightly whisk the eggs, keeping some visible white streaks.

3. In a medium skillet or shallow pot with a lid, combine the dashi and mirin and bring to a boil over medium-high heat. Reduce the heat to medium, stir in the soy sauce and onion, and bring to a simmer. Cook until the onion is starting to soften, 2 to 3 minutes. Add the chicken and stir to submerge it in the liquid as much as possible. Cook until the onion is soft and the chicken is cooked through, 3 to 4 minutes, turning the chicken pieces over after 2 minutes.

4. Reduce the heat to medium-low and bring to a gentle simmer. Working in a circular motion, drizzle two-thirds of the eggs over the chicken and onions, covering all the ingredients. Cover the skillet and cook until the eggs are barely set and still runny, 3 to 5 minutes. Uncover and drizzle the remaining eggs to fill the gaps or where the egg looks most cooked. Cook, uncovered, until the remaining eggs are slightly set, 2 to 4 minutes. If the eggs are not as set as you like after 4 minutes, cover with the lid again and cook to your desired doneness. Remove the skillet from the heat.

5. Sprinkle the scallion slices over the chicken-egg mixture. Divide the rice among four bowls and spoon the egg-chicken mixture over the rice.

tips | Sogi giri is a Japanese technique of cutting meat thinly with the knife at an angle to the cutting board; this increases the surface area of each piece. Use a long, sharp knife and cut in long strokes. This allows the meat to cook quickly, which works especially well for oyako don.

• Do not overmix the eggs. I like keeping some egg white streaks for a more interesting texture.

Soboro Don

そぼろ丼

Soboro don always reminds me of spring, even though you can eat it year-round. Maybe because of the snow peas, which are extra sweet in the spring. I grew up mostly eating soboro don as a donburi—in a deep bowl over rice—but I also enjoyed it as a bento. My mother would make the toppings the day before and store them in separate containers. I loved the surprise of opening my bento and seeing the beautiful, colorful arrangement of ingredients. Soboro refers to the finely ground texture of the chicken and egg. You can mix everything together as you eat, or you can keep the ingredients separate.

Serves 4

SNOW PEAS

1 cup snow peas or sugar snap peas

Kosher salt

CHICKEN SOBORO

1 pound ground chicken

¼ cup soy sauce

2 tablespoons sake

2 tablespoons mirin

1 teaspoon finely grated fresh ginger

EGG SOBORO

6 large eggs

1 tablespoon mirin

2 teaspoons sake

1 tablespoon sugar

¼ teaspoon kosher salt

1 teaspoon neutral oil, such as canola or grapeseed

4 cups freshly cooked rice (see page 115)

1. COOK THE SNOW PEAS: Using your fingertips, remove the stem and tough strings running along both sides of the snow peas. Bring a medium pot of salted water to a boil. Fill a large bowl with ice water. Add the snow peas to the boiling water and cook until bright-green and just tender, 2 to 3 minutes. Drain the snow peas and transfer to the bowl of ice water. Let cool for a few minutes, then drain the snow peas. Cut on a diagonal into ¼-inch-wide slices. Set aside.

2. MAKE THE CHICKEN SOBORO: In a shallow pot, combine the chicken, soy sauce, sake, mirin, and ginger. Set the pot over medium heat and using a wooden spatula or four chopsticks, stir and "cut" the mixture until it has a very fine texture (see Tip). Cook, stirring and "cutting" frequently, until the chicken is cooked through, 5 to 7 minutes. Set aside.

3. MAKE THE EGG SOBORO: In a medium bowl, whisk the eggs, mirin, sake, sugar, and salt. In a medium nonstick skillet, heat the oil over low heat. Add the egg mixture and cook, stirring with four chopsticks to make very finely scrambled eggs, until the eggs are set, 4 to 6 minutes. Make sure the eggs don't brown.

4. To assemble, place 1 cup of rice in each of four deep bowls. Dividing evenly among the bowls, cover one-third of the rice with chicken, one-third with eggs, and the remaining third with the snow peas. Eat with a spoon.

tips | The trick to achieving a very fine, crumbly texture for the chicken and eggs is to stir with four chopsticks as they cook. Use chopsticks with the pointiest tips for the best results. You can also use a wooden spatula to stir and "cut" the mixture.

• If you can't find fresh snow peas or sugar snap peas, you can substitute green beans or frozen peas.

Salmon Rice Bowl

鮭の混ぜご飯

I ate this rice bowl for lunch almost every day when I worked long hours in restaurant kitchens. I'd make a large batch of the key components—salmon flakes, pickled radish, and radish greens—and store them in the refrigerator for several days. Then I'd quickly assemble the bowl and eat it right before working a shift. It was a nourishing and filling meal, with a balance of rice, vegetables, and protein. Over time, it became one of my favorite meals and the recipe I chose for my first Tasty Japan video at BuzzFeed. The method I use for cooking salmon is similar to poaching the fish in a concentrated sake-mirin sauce. The liquid entirely evaporates while the salmon absorbs all of the flavors. If you're short on time, you can make a simplified version with just salmon flakes mixed with rice and some lightly dressed greens (see Tip on page 126).

Serves 4

PICKLED RADISH

1 bunch of radishes (about 10½ ounces), cut into quarters (greens reserved)

½ cup distilled white vinegar

½ cup dry white wine

3 tablespoons sugar

1 teaspoon kosher salt

SALMON FLAKES

¼ cup sake

¼ cup mirin

8 ounces skinless salmon

2 teaspoons toasted sesame oil

1 teaspoon kosher salt, plus more to taste

RADISH GREENS

Kosher salt

Radish greens from 1 bunch, washed well

FOR SERVING

4 cups freshly cooked rice (see page 115)

1 avocado, halved and sliced

4 fried eggs

Sriracha (optional)

1. MAKE THE PICKLED RADISH: Place the radish quarters in a large sterilized glass jar (about 32 ounces); see Tip on page 126. In a small pot, combine ½ cup water, the vinegar, white wine, sugar, and salt. Bring to a boil over high heat and cook, stirring, until the sugar and salt are completely dissolved, about 2 minutes. Pour immediately into the jar, covering the radishes. Let cool to room temperature, close the jar with a lid, and store in the refrigerator for 30 minutes and up to 3 months.

2. MAKE THE SALMON FLAKES: In a medium skillet with a lid, combine ¼ cup water, the sake, and mirin. Add the salmon and bring to a boil over medium heat. Reduce the heat to medium-low, cover and cook at a gentle simmer until the liquid has reduced by about half, 5 to 7 minutes. Uncover and continue cooking, using a wooden spatula to break the salmon into smaller pieces, until the liquid has evaporated and the salmon is cooked through, 4 to 6 minutes. If the salmon is cooked through but there is still liquid, increase the heat to medium and cook until it evaporates completely.

(recipe continues)

3. Add the sesame oil and stir well to combine. Remove the skillet from the heat and add the salt. Stir to combine and taste the salmon, seasoning with more salt, if needed. (The salmon should be well seasoned since it will be mixed in with rice.) Set aside. The salmon flakes will keep in an airtight container in the refrigerator for up to 5 days.

4. COOK THE RADISH GREENS:
Bring a small pot of salted water to a boil. Add the radish greens and cook until bright green, about 1 minute. Drain and rinse under cold water. Squeeze out the water, then sprinkle with 1 teaspoon salt and set aside for 5 minutes. Squeeze again, then roughly chop. Set aside. Cooked radish greens will keep in an airtight container in the refrigerator for up to 5 days.

5. TO SERVE: In a large bowl, combine the rice, salmon flakes, and radish greens. Wet a rice paddle or large spoon with water (so the rice doesn't stick) and mix in a cutting motion to avoid smashing the rice grains. Divide the rice mixture among four bowls. Top each with pickled radish, sliced avocado, and a fried egg. Drizzle with sriracha, if desired.

tips | Choose radishes that have fresh vibrant greens since you'll be using them in the recipe (avoid radish bunches with wilted, yellowed leaves). If you can't find radishes with nice greens, you can replace with spinach or arugula lightly dressed with oil and vinegar or a squeeze of lemon.

• Radishes and their greens need to be cleaned to remove any dirt and sand. I usually soak them in water for a few minutes, then rinse under running water.

• If you can, make the pickled radish a day in advance so that it is more fully pickled.

• To sterilize a jar, bring a large pot of water to a boil and boil the jar and lid for 1 minute. Let the jar and lid air-dry.

Katsu Don

カツ丼

Sliced pork cutlets simmered in eggs and dashi and served over rice—known as katsu don—is perfect for using leftover tonkatsu. If you've already made the pork cutlets, you can cook this dish in under 30 minutes. I often ate katsu don as a college student because of how filling it is. It had everything I craved at that age—fried pork, soft eggs, rice—minus the vegetables. It's still my go-to recipe when I'm hungry and need to use up leftover pork cutlets. You can eat it as a one-bowl meal or serve it with the Cabbage Salad with Lemon-Miso Dressing (page 54), Quick Pickles (page 94), or the Loaded Vegetable Miso Soup (page 34).

Serves 4

4 large eggs

⅔ cup awase or kombu dashi, instant or homemade (see page 32)

3 tablespoons mirin

3 tablespoons soy sauce

½ yellow onion, thinly sliced (about 1 cup)

4 Tonkatsu (page 87), cut into 1-inch slices

1 scallion, thinly sliced

4 cups freshly cooked rice (see page 115)

1. Crack the eggs into a large measuring cup, a small pitcher, or a medium bowl. Lightly whisk the eggs, keeping some visible white streaks.

2. In a medium skillet or shallow pot with a lid, combine the dashi and mirin and bring to a boil over medium-high heat. Reduce the heat to medium, stir in the soy sauce and onion, and bring to a simmer. Cook until the onion is starting to soften, 3 to 5 minutes. Reduce the heat to medium-low (the cooking liquid should still be at a slight simmer). Add the fried pork cutlets on top.

3. Working in a circular motion, drizzle two-thirds of the eggs over the pork and onions, covering all the ingredients. Cover the skillet and cook until the eggs are barely set and still runny, 3 to 5 minutes. Remove the lid and drizzle the remaining eggs to fill the gaps or where the egg looks most cooked. Cook, uncovered, until the remaining eggs are slightly set, 2 to 4 minutes. If the eggs are not as set as you like after 4 minutes, cover with the lid again and cook to your desired doneness. Remove the skillet from the heat.

4. Sprinkle the scallion slices over the pork-egg mixture. Divide the rice among four bowls and spoon the mixture over the rice.

Taco Rice

タコライス

My husband and I rarely cook together because I do most of the cooking at home. In fact, the two recipes he ever cooks are tacos and roast chicken. For my birthday, he'll always ask: Do you want tacos or chicken? One reason I love taco night is for the leftovers and the taco rice I'll assemble the next day. It's also a nice change to be in the kitchen side by side. He'll prepare the taco meat while I make the salsa and guacamole. Since we always keep some rice in the freezer (see page 117), this recipe comes together easily with taco-filling leftovers. On a busy day, I'll use store-bought salsa to save time. I recently discovered that taco rice is a popular dish in Okinawa, where there are many American military bases. Since my husband is from Texas, this Tex-Mex-Japanese food is perfect for us.

Serves 4

TACO SEASONING

1 tablespoon smoked paprika

2 teaspoons ground cumin

1 teaspoon crushed red pepper flakes

¼ teaspoon garlic powder

¼ teaspoon onion powder

½ teaspoon dried oregano

¼ teaspoon cayenne pepper

1 teaspoon kosher salt

Freshly ground black pepper

MEAT

1 tablespoon neutral oil, such as canola or grapeseed

½ yellow onion, cut into ½-inch pieces

1 green bell pepper, cut into ½-inch pieces

1 pound ground beef (90% lean)

Kosher salt

FOR SERVING

2 cups hot cooked rice (see page 115)

4 fried eggs

1 avocado, sliced

½ head romaine lettuce, thinly sliced

½ cup fresh cilantro leaves

Salsa, homemade (recipe follows) or store-bought

tip | You can use any kind of store-bought taco seasoning if you don't have time to make the homemade seasoning. Follow the directions on the seasoning packet for the amount.

1. MAKE THE TACO SEASONING: In a small bowl, combine the smoked paprika, cumin, pepper flakes, garlic powder, onion powder, oregano, cayenne pepper, salt, and black pepper to taste. Stir well and set aside.

2. COOK THE MEAT: In a medium skillet, heat the oil over medium-high heat. Add the onion and bell pepper and cook, stirring, until softened, about 5 minutes. Add the ground beef and cook, breaking apart the beef with the back of a wooden spoon or spatula, until browned, about 10 minutes. Sprinkle the taco seasoning over the beef and stir well. Add ⅓ cup water and bring to a simmer. Reduce the heat to medium and cook, stirring occasionally, until all the water has evaporated, about 10 minutes. Taste and season with more salt, if needed.

3. TO SERVE: Divide the rice among four bowls. Top with the taco meat, fried egg, avocado, romaine lettuce, and cilantro leaves. Drizzle with about 1 tablespoon salsa and serve.

Salsa

Makes about 2 cups

3 tomatoes on the vine, cut into 1-inch cubes

1 jalapeño, seeded and deribbed

1 garlic clove, peeled

1 teaspoon ground cumin

½ teaspoon kosher salt

In a food processor or blender, combine the tomatoes, jalapeño, garlic, cumin, and salt. Pulse or blend until all the ingredients are finely chopped. Transfer to a bowl. The salsa will keep in an airtight container in the refrigerator for up to 2 days.

Omurice

オムライス

You might have seen images or videos of omurice—rice covered with an omelet—from Kichi Kichi, the famous yoshoku restaurant in Kyoto. Chef Motokichi's omurice is a perfect fluffy omelet served over fried rice. When Chef Motokichi slits open the omelet, runny scrambled egg oozes out as the omelet unfolds and wraps around the rice. It's a beautiful dish; however, the omurice I grew up eating is a simple "chicken rice" (chicken fried rice seasoned with ketchup) wrapped in a thin omelet with a big dollop of ketchup on top. It's one of my favorite childhood dishes, and so delicious. I just love the pairing of sweet ketchup rice with a soft omelet draped over. If you are making more than two portions of ketchup rice, it's easier to cook the rice in an electric rice cooker. If wrapping the rice with an omelet feels too intimidating, you can simply place the omelet on top of the rice and make an "open-faced" omurice—it will taste delicious either way.

Serves 4

KETCHUP RICE

1½ cups short-grain rice

4 slices bacon (4 ounces total), cut into ½-inch pieces

½ yellow onion, finely chopped (about ½ cup)

¼ cup ketchup

1 teaspoon Worcestershire sauce

¼ teaspoon kosher salt

1 bay leaf

1 tablespoon unsalted butter

OMELETS

8 large eggs

Kosher salt and freshly ground black pepper

4 tablespoons (½ stick) unsalted butter

Ketchup, for topping

1. MAKE THE KETCHUP RICE: Wash the rice (see Washing Rice, page 116) and drain. In a bowl, cover the rice with 1 inch of water and soak for 30 minutes. Drain the rice and put it in a rice cooker's inner pot, a Dutch oven, or a medium pot with a tight-fitting lid.

2. Place the bacon in a cold medium skillet. Turn the heat to medium and cook the bacon until slightly crispy at the edges, about 8 minutes. Add the onion and cook, stirring, until soft, about 3 minutes. Set aside.

3. To the rice, add 1½ cups water, the ketchup, Worcestershire sauce, and salt. Stir with chopsticks or a fork to combine the ingredients. Place the bacon, onion, and bay leaf on top of the rice. Do not stir. If using an electric rice cooker, close the lid and choose the setting for regular white rice. If using a Dutch oven or medium pot, follow the stovetop directions for cooking rice on page 118.

4. When the rice is cooked, add the butter and mix well with a rice paddle or a spatula. Discard the bay leaf.

5. MAKE THE OMELETS: Crack 2 eggs into a small bowl. Add 1 tablespoon water and season with salt and pepper. Mix well with chopsticks or a fork until the egg whites are fully blended with the yolks.

6. In a nonstick medium skillet, melt 1 tablespoon of the butter over medium-low heat. Add the egg mixture and cook, mixing with a silicone spatula, until the mixture resembles soft-scrambled eggs and the bottom and edges are just set, about 3 minutes.

7. Add one-quarter of the ketchup rice (about 1 packed cup) to the center of the omelet. Fold both sides of the omelet over the rice to shape into a football, or fold one side over and roll the omelet over in the skillet. Slide onto a plate, seam-side down, so the rice isn't visible. (Alternatively, pack about 1 cup ketchup rice into a small bowl and then invert onto a plate. Slide the omelet on top of the mound of rice.) Repeat with the remaining butter, eggs, and rice.

8. Top each omelet with about 1 tablespoon ketchup (or more if desired) and serve.

Garlicky Egg Fried Rice with Bacon

チャーハン

Japanese fried rice, known as chāhan, is made with short-grain rice. I prefer a fried rice where the grains are fully separated. In Japanese, we call this para para (パラパラ). My secret to para para is combining the eggs and rice beforehand, so the egg coats each grain of rice as it cooks. The other secret is to avoid overcrowding the skillet. I use my biggest nonstick skillet and make two portions (3 cups of cooked rice) at the most. If you want to make a larger quantity, you can double the amounts in the ingredient list and cook the fried rice in two batches.

This fried rice gets tons of flavor from garlic, soy sauce, and butter. If you have leftover cooked rice, it comes together in under 30 minutes, making it the ideal quick lunch or dinner. I don't usually add a side dish, but if you want a more "balanced" meal, you could serve it with the Broccoli and Bean Salad (page 49) or a simple green salad.

Serves 2

3 cups cooked rice (see page 115), preferably day-old or cooled down

2 large eggs

2 slices bacon (2 ounces total), cut into 1-inch pieces

1 tablespoon neutral oil, such as canola or grapeseed

4 garlic cloves, finely chopped

3 scallions, thinly sliced

1 tablespoon plus 1 teaspoon soy sauce, plus more to taste

2 tablespoons unsalted butter

½ teaspoon kosher salt, plus more to taste

Freshly ground black pepper

1. In a large bowl, combine the rice and eggs. Using a rice paddle or spatula, mix well and set aside.

2. Line a plate with paper towels. Place the bacon in a cold large nonstick skillet. Turn on the heat to medium and cook, stirring occasionally, until the bacon is crispy, about 5 minutes. Using a slotted spoon, transfer the bacon to the paper towels to drain.

3. To the same skillet, add the oil, if needed. You want at least 1 tablespoon oil or bacon fat in the skillet. Set the skillet over medium heat, add the garlic, and cook until fragrant but not browned, about 2 minutes.

4. Increase the heat to high and add the egg-rice mixture. Cook, stirring frequently with a wooden spatula, until the rice grains are separated and the eggs start to set, about 5 minutes. Add two-thirds of the scallions and cook, stirring, for 3 minutes. (Reserve the remaining sliced scallions for garnish.) Add the soy sauce and butter. Cook, stirring, until the butter is completely melted, about 3 minutes. Add the bacon and stir to combine. Add the salt and season with pepper to taste. Taste and season with more soy sauce or salt, as needed.

5. Divide the rice between two bowls, garnish with the reserved sliced scallions, and serve immediately.

Corn Rice

とうもろこしご飯

The combination of soy sauce, butter, and corn in this dish reminds me of summer festivals in Japan. Many food vendors sell yaki tōmorokoshi, grilled corn that is brushed with soy sauce and butter. It's a golden combination: sweet, salty, and a bit caramelized. I recommend making this rice in the summer, during peak corn season, when it's sweetest and juiciest. I add the cob to the rice as it cooks so it infuses the dish with even more concentrated sweet corn flavor.

Serves 4

2 cups short-grain rice

1 ear corn, or about 1 cup corn kernels

2 teaspoons soy sauce

1 teaspoon kosher salt

1 tablespoon unsalted butter

tips | Use frozen corn if you can't find fresh.

• I also love the flavor combination of soy sauce and melted butter for seasoning popcorn.

• It's important to soak the rice first. The grains will look whiter when they've soaked up enough water. If you skip this step, the grains might not cook all the way through.

1. Wash the rice (see Washing Rice, page 116) and drain. Add the rice to a rice cooker's inner pot, Dutch oven, or large heavy pot with a tight-fitting lid. Add 2 cups water and soak for at least 30 minutes and up to 1 hour.

2. Using a sharp knife, cut the corn kernels from the cob. Reserve the cob.

3. To the rice, add 1 teaspoon of the soy sauce and the salt. Stir with chopsticks or a fork to combine the ingredients. Scatter the corn kernels over the rice, then place the cob on top. Do not stir. If using an electric rice cooker, close and choose the setting for regular rice. If cooking on the stove, cover the pot with the lid and bring to a boil over high heat. Reduce the heat to medium-low and cook, covered, for 17 minutes. Remove the pot from the heat and keep covered for 10 minutes. (Do not open the lid; the rice is steaming.)

4. Remove the cob and discard. Add the butter and remaining 1 teaspoon soy sauce. Using a rice paddle, mix well to evenly distribute the corn. Serve hot.

Mushroom and Carrot Mixed Rice

炊き込みご飯

Takikomi gohan, which loosely translates to "mixed rice" or "seasoned rice," reminds me of fall in Japan. Maybe because mushrooms are in season and it's a staple element for bentos that you'd bring along on hikes or picnics in the autumn, just as the leaves start to change color. This is also a one-pot, balanced meal, perfect for a weeknight. The mushrooms cook with the rice, infusing it with plenty of flavor, and there's a gentle sweetness from the carrot and dashi. Sometimes I have the Loaded Vegetable Miso Soup (page 34) on the side, but the rice is satisfying on its own.

Serves 4

2 cups short-grain rice

2⅓ cups awase or kombu dashi, instant or homemade (see page 32)

2 tablespoons soy sauce

Kosher salt

1 tablespoon sake

½ small carrot, cut into thin matchsticks (about ⅓ cup)

3 ounces oyster mushrooms, torn into bite-size pieces

3 ounces shimeji mushrooms, torn into bite-size pieces

½ cup frozen shelled edamame

1. Wash the rice (see Washing Rice, page 116) and drain. Add the rice to a rice cooker's inner pot, Dutch oven, or large heavy pot with a tight-fitting lid. Add the dashi and soak for 30 minutes to 1 hour.

2. To the rice, add the soy sauce, ½ teaspoon salt, and the sake. Stir with chopsticks or a fork to combine the ingredients. Place the carrot, oyster mushrooms, and shimeji mushrooms over the rice. Do not stir. If using an electric rice cooker, close and choose the setting for regular white rice. If using a Dutch oven or pot, cover the pot with a tight-fitting lid and bring to a boil over high heat. Reduce the heat to medium-low and cook, covered, for 17 minutes. Remove the pot from the heat and keep covered for 10 minutes. (Do not open the lid; the rice is steaming.)

3. Meanwhile, bring a medium pot of salted water to a boil. Add the edamame and cook until bright green and tender, about 5 minutes.

4. Add the edamame to the rice and mix well with a rice paddle. Serve hot or at room temperature.

tips | You can swap in different varieties of mushrooms, such as baby bella or shiitake for the shimeji.

• It's important to soak the rice first. The grains will look whiter when they've soaked up enough water. If you skip this step, the grains might not cook all the way through.

Onigiri
おにぎり

Onigiri or omusubi are small rice balls (about the size of a tennis ball). They are often covered in nori (seaweed) and hide a flavorful filling inside. It's one of the simplest and most accessible foods—in Japan, you can find them at most grocery stores, including 7-Elevens—but is also incredibly comforting and nourishing. There are many flavors, and here I'll share some of my favorites. Onigiri are easy to hold in your hands, making it the perfect travel food. Usually, it's the main component of a bento.

One of the most important rules for making onigiri is to use freshly cooked rice that is hot or very warm. It will be difficult to shape the onigiri when the rice is cold or at room temperature. I've always thought that making these rice balls is an act of love. As with other home cooking, you're preparing it for your family, friends, or yourself, but especially with onigiri, it feels extra intimate (and a bit painful!) since you're holding and shaping very hot rice with your bare hands. I think about this whenever I make onigiri for my son, Hugo, because they're his favorite food, and I'm reminded of my mom, who would make onigiri for me and my siblings all the time.

Makes 4

(recipe continues)

Salted Onigiri
塩むすび

tips | Make sure to have a bowl of water ready. I dip my hands in water before making each onigiri to prevent the rice from sticking to my hands.

• Do not press or pack the rice too much when you are shaping the onigiri. The rice grains should come apart in your mouth when you bite into it. Press just hard enough for the grains to stick together, but not so much that the onigiri will be dense.

• For nori (seaweed), I like using a seasoned kind called aji nori. It's slightly sweet and salty. It usually comes in a smaller package.

• I recommend using sea salt instead of kosher salt to season the rice. You'll notice the difference in flavor, especially for the shio musubi (salted rice ball).

• Each onigiri should be about 320 grams.

Shio musubi is a rice ball seasoned only with salt. I think the most common way to make onigiri is to wet your hands, spread some salt on your palms, and shape the onigiri, lightly seasoning the outside of the rice ball as you do so. However, my mom always mixed the salt into the rice for even seasoning, so this is also how I make my onigiri. Use this recipe as a base when you are making onigiri with a filling.

1¾ cups freshly cooked short-grain rice (see page 115)

¼ teaspoon fine sea salt

4 pieces nori (seaweed), preferably seasoned, about 2 × 4 inches

Place the rice in a medium bowl. Sprinkle with the salt and mix well using a wet rice paddle or spatula. Divide the rice into four equal portions. Lightly wet your hands and shape each portion into a 4-inch ball. Gently press the ball into a triangle-shaped puck. Wrap each one with a piece of nori.

Tuna Mayo Onigiri
ツナマヨおにぎり

This is my favorite konbini (convenience store) onigiri. They will be most flavorful if you use tuna packed in olive oil and Kewpie mayonnaise.

TUNA-MAYO FILLING

2 tablespoons canned tuna, preferably packed in olive oil

2 teaspoons mayonnaise, preferably Kewpie

1 teaspoon soy sauce

Pinch of kosher salt

RICE BALLS

1¾ cups freshly cooked short-grain rice (see page 115)

¼ teaspoon fine sea salt

4 pieces nori (seaweed), preferably seasoned, about 2 × 4 inches

1. MAKE THE TUNA-MAYO FILLING: In a small bowl, combine the tuna, mayonnaise, soy sauce, and kosher salt.

2. MAKE THE RICE BALLS: Place the rice in a medium bowl. Sprinkle with the sea salt and mix well using a wet rice paddle or spatula. Divide the rice into four equal portions. Lightly wet your hands. Take one portion of rice in your hand and make an indent in the middle. Place a heaping 1 teaspoon of the tuna-mayo filling in the indent. Wrap the rice around the filling and shape it into a 4-inch-ball. Gently press the ball into a triangle-shaped puck. Wrap with a piece of nori. Repeat with the remaining ingredients.

Umeboshi Onigiri
梅干しおにぎり

Umeboshi—pickled plum—is a classic onigiri filling that is very salty and sour. Just a small amount provides a ton of flavor. There are different kinds of umeboshi at Japanese grocery stores. My favorite is made with honey because it's milder. Umeboshi also comes in various sizes, so if your umeboshi are big, use half per onigiri.

1¾ cups freshly cooked short-grain rice (see page 115)

¼ teaspoon fine sea salt

2 to 4 umeboshi, pitted

4 pieces nori (seaweed), preferably seasoned, about 2 × 4 inches

Place the rice in a medium bowl. Sprinkle with the salt and mix well using a wet rice paddle or spatula. Divide the rice into four equal portions. Lightly wet your hands. Take one portion of rice in your hand and make an indent in the middle. If your umeboshi are large, place half of one in the indent; if they are small, use a whole umeboshi. Wrap the rice around the filling and shape into a 4-inch-ball. Gently press the ball into a triangle-shaped puck. Wrap with a piece of nori. Repeat with the remaining ingredients.

(recipe continues)

Mixed Sumac Onigiri
スマックのおにぎり

In Japan, you can find premade seasonings for rice. My favorite is yukari, which is made with dried salted red shiso leaves. It's salty and tangy, and similar to dried umeboshi. The flavor reminds me of sumac, so I started using sumac mixed with salt as an alternative.

2 teaspoons sumac

½ teaspoon fine sea salt

1¾ cups freshly cooked short-grain rice (see page 115)

1. In a small bowl, mix the sumac and salt.

2. Place the rice in a medium bowl. Sprinkle the sumac-salt over the rice. Using a wet rice paddle or spatula, mix to combine. Working one at a time, lightly wet your hands and shape the rice mixture into four 4-inch-balls, gently pressing the balls into triangle-shaped pucks.

Yaki Onigiri
焼きおにぎり

I love the crunchy, toasted flavor of yaki onigiri, a rice ball cooked in a hot pan. It reminds me of the crispy rice at the bottom of a pot. Yaki onigiri should be eaten right away, while it's still warm and crisp.

1¾ cups freshly cooked short-grain rice (see page 115)

2 tablespoons soy sauce

2 teaspoons mirin

1 teaspoon toasted sesame oil

1. In a medium bowl, using a wet rice paddle or spatula, mix the rice with the soy sauce, mirin, and sesame oil.

2. Divide the rice into four equal portions. Place one portion of rice on a piece of plastic wrap. Using the plastic, shape the rice into a 4-inch-ball. Gently press the ball into a triangle-shaped puck. (You don't have to use plastic wrap, but it'll be harder to shape without it.) Repeat to make four onigiri.

3. Heat a cast-iron pan or nonstick skillet over medium heat. Add the onigiri and cook on both sides until crispy and golden brown, about 3 minutes per side. Serve hot.

Bonito and Sesame Furikake

ふりかけ

Furikake is a dry seasoning that can be sprinkled over rice. There are many flavors of it, but my favorite is this classic katsuo furikake that's made with bonito flakes. You can find it at most grocery stores these days, as well as online, but since it has become my son's favorite seasoning, I started making it from scratch. I love to make a simple shio musubi (Salted Onigiri, page 140) and sprinkle the furikake on top.

Makes 1 cup

¼ cup (2g) bonito flakes

¼ cup toasted white sesame seeds

1 teaspoon sugar

¼ teaspoon fine sea salt

1 teaspoon toasted sesame oil

1 teaspoon soy sauce

10 sheets (about 5g) nori (seaweed)

1. Place the bonito flakes in a small bowl. Using your fingers, crumble it very finely.

2. In a small skillet, combine the bonito flakes, sesame seeds, sugar, salt, sesame oil, soy sauce, and 2 teaspoons water. Cook over medium-low heat until dry and crumbly, about 2 minutes. Set aside.

3. In a small bowl, crumble the seaweed sheets into small pieces. Add the bonito flake mixture to the bowl and mix to combine. The furikake will keep in an airtight container in the refrigerator for up to 2 weeks.

how to build a bento

Bento means "boxed lunch" in Japanese. My mom made bentos for me and my siblings almost every day when we were in high school. Usually, they contained a combination of leftovers from dinner and something fresh she had cooked in the morning. She would purposely set aside extra food from dinner for our bentos. For example, when we had tempura or croquettes, she would make smaller ones or bake a little gratin in muffin tins to better fit inside a bento box. Here are a few important guidelines for packing a bento:

- Don't choose anything saucy or soupy, to prevent leaking.
- Avoid ingredients bathed in a broth or sauce, such as braised fish or salads that release a lot of liquid, like the Cucumber and Fennel Sunomono (page 53).
- Avoid raw fish. In general, I try to avoid any ingredient that needs to be refrigerated up until the moment it's eaten, as a bento should be somewhat "shelf-stable" for a few hours.
- Think about the colors of your assortment. Part of the pleasure of building a bento is creating a beautiful lunch. Many bento items tend to be brown or beige. If that's the case, add a few colorful vegetables, such as cherry tomatoes or blanched broccoli or snap peas.

When choosing your bento box or vessel, of which there are many different kinds (plastic, wooden, glass, or stainless steel), think about the size, specifically how much you'd like to put in the bento depending on how much you eat. I usually pick a container that doesn't have too many compartments, which gives me more flexibility for the dishes. The ingredients themselves can create separation between the dishes, like using broccoli or tomatoes to separate dishes, or you can use small muffin cups. When I was in high school, my mom would wrap my bento box in a large cloth or handkerchief to create a tighter seal, to catch any leakage, and to use as a napkin.

(recipe continues)

TO PACK A BENTO: Fill half of your bento box with rice items, such as Onigiri (rice balls, page 138), Corn Rice (page 134), or Mushroom and Carrot Mixed Rice (page 137). You could also just add white rice topped with umeboshi (pickled plum) or furikake, a flavorful dried condiment that you can find at Asian or Japanese grocery stores (see the recipe for homemade furikake on page 143). If you're feeling ambitious, you can cut out shapes from a piece of nori (seaweed) to make a bento character (kyaraben) using the white rice as a base. (My mom would often make Hello Kitty for me.) Then pack one protein dish (fish or meat), one slice of rolled omelet (Tamagoyaki, page 84), and a vegetable side.

When I was in high school, there was no refrigerator to store our bentos, so we would keep them at room temperature for a few hours.

Traditionally, the food is well seasoned and therefore a bit preserved. As long as the bento is kept in a cool, dark place, it should be fine for a few hours. That said, if you're worried about food safety, you can refrigerate it. Ideally remove it from the fridge 30 or so minutes before eating so that everything is at room temperature; it will taste better that way.

Here are three "bento menus," though I encourage you to play around with other recipes in the book, mixing and matching to find your favorite combinations:

Both the Omurice (page 130) and Soboro Don (page 123) work perfectly for a bento. For the omurice, I usually add a squeeze of ketchup over the rice, and then I cover it with the omelet, so the ketchup doesn't smear onto the bento lid.

Fried Chicken Bento

Karaage (page 62)

Slice of Tamagoyaki (page 84)

Potato Salad (page 50)

Cherry tomato

Mushroom and Carrot Mixed Rice (page 137) or white rice with Bonito and Sesame Furikake (page 143)

Shrimp Kakiage Bento

Shrimp and Mixed Vegetable Kakiage (page 109)

Slice of Tamagoyaki (chive variation; see Tip, page 86)

Soy Sauce–Simmered Kabocha (page 38)

Blanched broccoli

Onigiri (page 138)

Veggie Bento

Curried Kabocha Croquette (page 46)

Swiss chard from the miso-marinated cod (page 101)

Roasted Cauliflower Goma-ae (page 41)

Blanched snap peas

Corn Rice (page 134)

noodles

Easy Soy Sauce Ramen

簡単醤油ラーメン

In Japan, ramen is one of those meals I usually eat out because it's affordable and can be labor-intensive to make from scratch. I've noticed that ramen has become very popular in the US, especially the kind made with tonkotsu (pork broth). However, I prefer a lighter broth, such as shio (salt) or shoyu (soy sauce), which can be harder to find in restaurants here. So, for this book, I set out to make my own recipe with a shoyu broth—one that would be worthy of a restaurant meal while being quick and easy to cook at home. This recipe almost feels like cheating because it's so delicious despite using all pantry ingredients for the broth. It may seem like a lot of scallion-garlic oil, but there's no other fat in the broth aside from a bit of butter, and it'll round out the flavor of the dish. Don't worry if you don't have time to make braised pork belly or seasoned eggs. This ramen is equally delicious with sautéed cabbage and bean sprouts, or just a soft-boiled egg.

Serves 4

SCALLION-GARLIC OIL

2 scallions, thinly sliced

4 garlic cloves, thinly sliced

½ cup neutral oil, such as canola or grapeseed

BROTH

4 cups clam juice (see Tip)

4 cups chicken broth

2 tablespoons soy sauce

1 teaspoon kosher salt, plus more to taste

FOR SERVING

4 teaspoons toasted sesame oil

20 ounces fresh ramen noodles

4 Soft-Boiled Eggs (see Tip; recipe follows)

16 slices Chā Shū (braised pork belly, optional, page 80)

1 scallion, thinly sliced

2 tablespoons unsalted butter, cut into 4 equal slices

tips | Try to find clam juice in a glass bottle. Clam juice in a can might have a slight metallic flavor.

• If you can't find ramen noodles, use the Spaghetti Baking Soda Hack (page 155).

1. Bring a large pot of water to a boil.

2. MAKE THE SCALLION-GARLIC OIL: In a small skillet, combine the scallions, garlic, and neutral oil. Cook over low heat until the garlic turns golden, about 15 minutes. Set aside.

3. MAKE THE BROTH: In a medium pot, combine the clam juice and chicken broth. Bring to a boil over medium-high heat and remove the pot from the heat. Add the soy sauce and salt and stir to combine. Taste and season with more salt, if desired. Cover and keep warm over low heat.

4. TO SERVE: Divide the scallion-garlic oil among four deep bowls. Add 1 teaspoon sesame oil to each bowl.

5. When the water is boiling, add the ramen noodles and cook according to the package directions. Drain the noodles and divide among the four bowls.

6. To each bowl, add about 2 cups of the broth. Halve the soft-boiled eggs. Top each bowl with the braised pork belly (if using), eggs, chopped scallion, and a slice of butter.

tips | The saltiness of
clam juice and chicken
broth varies depending on
the brand, so make sure
to taste the broth and
adjust the amount of salt
to your liking.

• For the soft-boiled eggs:
If you choose to use the
chā shū, that recipe has the
option of seasoning soft-
boiled eggs with the pork.
In that case, use those soft-
boiled eggs for the ramen.

Soft-Boiled Eggs
半熟卵

4 large eggs, at room
temperature

Fill a large bowl with water and ice. Bring a
medium pot of water to a boil, then reduce
to a simmer. Using a large spoon, gently add
the eggs one at a time. Cook for 7 minutes.
Transfer the eggs to the bowl with ice water.
Peel when ready to serve.

Kitsune Udon

きつねうどん

In Japan, there's a saying that aburaage (fried tofu pouches) are the favorite food of shrine foxes, so this dish, featuring braised aburaage, is called kitsune udon, or "fox udon." Kitsune udon is a simple and humble bowl of noodles in a light broth. I often crave it after a long flight or when I'm feeling under the weather. Because there are so few ingredients, the dashi is an essential component, and I recommend making it from scratch. If you can find usukuchi shoyu, a lighter-colored soy sauce, use it for a clearer broth.

Serves 4

BRAISED ABURAAGE

4 aburaage (fried tofu pouches)

1 cup homemade dashi, preferably awase (see page 33)

2 tablespoons soy sauce

1 tablespoon mirin

1 teaspoon sugar

BROTH

8 cups homemade dashi, preferably awase (see page 33)

½ cup soy sauce

¼ cup mirin

¼ cup sake

FOR SERVING

14 ounces (4 bundles) dried udon noodles or 30 ounces fresh or frozen udon noodles

Sliced scallions, for garnish

1. MAKE THE BRAISED ABURAAGE: Make a parchment cartouche (see page 23) that fits inside a small pot.

2. Fill the small pot halfway with water and bring to a boil over high heat. Add the aburaage and simmer for 2 minutes. (This is to remove some of the oil.) Drain in a colander and rinse under running water. Once cool to the touch, squeeze out the water with your fingers, being careful not to tear the pouch. Set aside and rinse the pot.

3. In the same pot, combine the aburaage, dashi, soy sauce, mirin, and sugar. Bring to a boil over medium-high heat, then reduce the heat to medium-low. Place the parchment cartouche on top and cook until the braising liquid is reduced and almost entirely absorbed by the tofu, about 15 minutes. (You should have 2 or 3 tablespoons of liquid left in the pot.) Remove the pot from the heat and keep covered. If not using right away, keep the cartouche on top and refrigerate for up to 3 days. Gently reheat on the stovetop before using.

4. MAKE THE BROTH: In a medium pot, combine the dashi, soy sauce, mirin, and sake. Bring to a boil over high heat and then reduce the heat to low to keep warm. The broth will keep in an airtight container in the refrigerator for up to 3 days and in the freezer for up to 3 months.

5. TO SERVE: Bring a large pot of water to a boil. Add the udon noodles and cook according to the package directions. Drain and divide among four bowls.

6. Add 2 cups of broth to each bowl. Add the braised aburaage, garnish with sliced scallions, and serve.

Yakisoba

やきそば

My grandmother's kissaten (Japanese tearoom and café) served yakisoba—pan-fried noodles coated in a slightly sweet, savory sauce—on a sizzling plate, and whenever I cook yakisoba today, the smell reminds me of my childhood and all the hours spent with her at the kissaten. It's a quick meal that you can throw together in 30 minutes, making it perfect for a weekday lunch or dinner. The fried egg is optional but highly recommended as the runny yolk becomes part of the sauce and adds a delicious richness. Yakisoba noodles can be found at Japanese or Asian grocery stores, and you can also buy premade yakisoba sauce, but I'm never able to finish the bottle before it expires. So I've started making my own with pantry items.

Yakisoba is traditionally made with thinly sliced pork belly, which is harder to find in the US. I use bacon instead, which makes the dish a bit saltier. Make sure to taste as you season with salt.

Serves 4

YAKISOBA SAUCE

¼ cup soy sauce

2 tablespoons Worcestershire sauce

2 tablespoons mirin

1 tablespoon hoisin sauce

NOODLES

8 slices bacon (8 ounces total), cut into 1-inch pieces

4 scallions, thinly sliced, white and green parts separated

2 carrots, thinly sliced on a diagonal

1 yellow onion, thinly sliced (about 2 cups)

½ pound green cabbage, cut into 1-inch pieces (about 2 cups)

Kosher salt and freshly ground black pepper

22 ounces fresh yakisoba, chow mein, or ramen noodles (see Spaghetti Baking Soda Hack; recipe follows)

4 fried eggs (optional), for serving

tips | When you cook bacon, start with a cold skillet. This way, you can slowly render the fat and the bacon becomes evenly crispy.

• It's important to cook the vegetables and noodles separately to avoid overcrowding the skillet.

1. MAKE THE YAKISOBA SAUCE: In a small bowl, combine the soy sauce, Worcestershire sauce, mirin, and hoisin sauce. Set aside.

2. MAKE THE NOODLES: Add the bacon to a cold large nonstick skillet. Turn the heat to medium-high and cook until the bacon is crispy, about 4 minutes. Transfer the bacon to a medium bowl.

3. To the same skillet, add the scallion whites and cook until fragrant, about 2 minutes. Add the carrots and onion and cook until the onion is translucent, about 1 minute. Add the cabbage and scallion greens and cook until soft, about 2 minutes. Season with salt and pepper. Transfer the vegetables to the bowl with the bacon.

4. To the same skillet, add the yakisoba noodles, stirring to separate the noodles. Cook until slightly crispy, about 3 minutes. Add the yakisoba sauce and toss to combine. Return the vegetables and bacon to the skillet and toss to combine.

5. Divide the noodles among four bowls. If desired, top each one with a fried egg.

Spaghetti Baking Soda Hack

If you can't find fresh yakisoba or ramen noodles, try my spaghetti baking soda hack: Add baking soda to the pasta water, which will turn spaghetti a shade darker and provide the flavor and springy texture of ramen.

1. Bring a large pot of salted water to a boil. Add 2 tablespoons baking soda and 8 ounces dried spaghetti and cook until al dente according to the package directions. Drain the spaghetti and rinse well under cold running water.

2. When cooking the spaghetti, place chopsticks or a wooden spoon over the pot. It'll keep the water from boiling over the edges of the pot. (When you add baking soda to the water, the water will boil over even more.)

Spicy Tuna Mazemen

スパイシーツナまぜ麺

I first encountered this no-broth ramen dish, called mazemen, through my friend Yuji Haraguchi. We met in NYC when I was working at Korin and Yuji was a fish distributor. Whenever I ran into him, he would talk about wanting to open a ramen shop. Two years later, he quit his day job to run a ramen pop-up in Brooklyn. His ramen was so popular that he asked if I could help as a server, so I worked with him at night and on the weekends. Because of his experience as a fishmonger, Yuji's ramen was unlike the heavy, pork-based preparations we often find in the US. He made a light broth with fish bones, used less meat, and focused on fresh vegetables. Eventually, he opened his first brick-and-mortar restaurant in Brooklyn called Okonomi, and today his empire has expanded to Japan and Thailand. My recipe for spicy tuna mazemen is inspired by Yuji's ramen and is an ode to his truly unique creations. Just make sure to mix everything together before eating.

Serves 4

SPICY TUNA

1 (5-ounce) can tuna in extra-virgin olive oil, drained

1 tablespoon thinly sliced chives

2 teaspoons shichimi togarashi, plus more to taste

TOPPINGS

2 Persian (mini) cucumbers

1 avocado

NOODLES

20 ounces fresh ramen noodles (see Tip)

¼ cup toasted sesame oil

FOR SERVING

½ cup Sweet Soy Sauce (recipe follows)

Sliced nori (seaweed)

Garlic chips (optional; from Rib-Eye Steak recipe, page 75)

tips | Yuji makes confit tuna from scratch, but I use canned tuna for this recipe. I recommend buying chunky tuna in extra-virgin olive oil.

• For ramen noodles, I like Sun Noodle's kaedama noodles. They're easy to find at grocery stores in LA (sometimes they're in the frozen aisle), but if you can't find them, try my Spaghetti Baking Soda Hack (page 155).

1. Bring a large pot of water to a boil.

2. MAKE THE SPICY TUNA: In a small bowl, combine the tuna, chives, and shichimi togarashi. Using a rubber spatula, gently toss and stir the ingredients, trying not to break apart the tuna too much. Taste and add more shichimi togarashi, if desired, depending on your spice preference.

3. PREPARE THE TOPPINGS: Thinly slice the cucumbers on a diagonal, then cut the slices lengthwise into thin matchsticks. Cut the avocado into quarters, then thinly slice.

4. COOK THE NOODLES: Once the water is boiling, add the ramen noodles and cook according to the package directions. Drain and rinse well under cold running water, using your hands to separate the strands. Shake the sieve to remove excess water.

5. Transfer the noodles to a medium bowl and add the sesame oil and stir to coat.

(recipe continues)

6. TO SERVE: Divide the noodles among four bowls. Drizzle each portion of noodles with 2 tablespoons of the sweet soy sauce. Top the noodles with the spicy tuna mixture, avocado, cucumbers, nori, and garlic chips (if using). Serve immediately and mix all the components right before eating.

tips | You can play around with the toppings. I also love the combination of sautéed kale, poached egg, and shredded nori.

• If you can't find shichimi togarashi, use cayenne pepper or chili oil to taste. (Cayenne pepper will be spicier than shichimi togarashi, so start with ½ teaspoon and add more depending on your preference.)

Sweet Soy Sauce

You can substitute the kombu and bonito flakes with 1 teaspoon of instant dashi. Add it to the sake in step 1 when you would add the kombu.

Makes about 1 cup

½ cup sake

1 (2-inch) square piece kombu

½ cup (4g) bonito flakes

¼ cup sugar

1½ tablespoons rice vinegar

1 teaspoon kosher salt

½ cup soy sauce

1. In a medium saucepan, combine the sake and kombu. Set aside at room temperature for 30 minutes.

2. Bring the sake and kombu to a boil over high heat, then remove the kombu. Add the bonito flakes, reduce the heat to medium-low, and simmer for 2 minutes. Remove the saucepan from the heat.

3. Add the sugar, rice vinegar, and salt to the saucepan and stir to dissolve the sugar. Stir in the soy sauce. Strain the sauce through a fine-mesh sieve to remove the bonito flakes. The sauce will keep in an airtight container in the refrigerator for up to 1 month.

Creamy Soy Milk Udon
with Pork and Bok Choy
豆乳とごまの冷やしうどん

This udon noodle recipe is not very traditional, but it's an easy and refreshing meal for the summer. It has a delicious creaminess from the tahini but remains light from the soy milk. The soy milk mixture is between a soup and a sauce—you'll have more liquid than in mazemen, but less than with a ramen in broth. Make sure to mix all the ingredients together in your bowl before digging in—the meat is very flavorful and will season the noodles. I also love to use this pork topping as a filling for Onigiri (page 138).

Serves 4

SOUP

1 cup unsweetened soy milk

1 tablespoon miso

3 tablespoons tahini

3 tablespoons toasted sesame oil

1 tablespoon soy sauce

2 tablespoons toasted white sesame seeds, coarsely ground (see Tip, page 41)

TOPPINGS

1 tablespoon toasted sesame oil

1 tablespoon soy sauce

1 tablespoon miso

1 teaspoon sugar

1 tablespoon plus 1 teaspoon neutral oil, such as canola or grapeseed

1 pound ground pork

1 garlic clove, finely grated

1 teaspoon finely grated fresh ginger

Kosher salt

1 bok choy, cut on a diagonal into 2-inch slices (about 1½ cups)

14 ounces (4 bundles) dried udon noodles or 30 ounces fresh or frozen udon noodles

1 tablespoon chili oil, or to taste

1. Bring a large pot of water to a boil.

2. MAKE THE SOUP: In a medium bowl, combine ¼ cup of the soy milk and the miso. Whisk to completely dissolve the miso. Add the remaining ¾ cup soy milk, the tahini, sesame oil, soy sauce, and sesame seeds. Whisk until combined. Refrigerate while you make the toppings.

3. MAKE THE TOPPINGS: In a small bowl, combine the sesame oil, soy sauce, miso, and sugar. Whisk well to dissolve the miso. Set aside.

4. In a medium skillet, heat 1 tablespoon of the neutral oil over medium-high heat. Add the ground pork and cook, breaking up the pork with the back of a spoon, until browned, about 10 minutes. Add the garlic and ginger and cook, stirring, until fragrant, about 1 minute. Add the sesame oil–miso mixture and cook, stirring, until everything is combined and the pork is lightly caramelized in spots, 3 to 4 minutes. Taste and season with salt, if needed. Transfer to a bowl.

(recipe continues)

5. Wipe the skillet clean, set it over medium-high heat, and add the remaining 1 teaspoon neutral oil. Add the bok choy and season with salt. Cook, stirring, until the leaves are slightly wilted and the stems are lightly browned, about 3 minutes.

6. Add the udon noodles to the pot of boiling water and cook according to the package directions. Drain and rinse well under cold water.

7. Divide the noodles among four bowls. Pour about ⅓ cup of the soup into each bowl of noodles. Top with the ground pork and bok choy. Drizzle with the chili oil, using more or less depending on your heat preference. Serve immediately.

tips | For a vegan version, use crumbled firm tofu or a plant-based ground meat instead of pork.

• Unlike for pasta, you don't need to add salt to the water when cooking udon.

• You can make the toppings and soup ahead of time and cook the noodles right before serving. Make sure to reheat the ground pork before serving.

Camembert Cheese Mazemen
with Prosciutto
カマンベールチーズのまぜ麺

This is another recipe inspired by Yuji Haraguchi's ramen (see page 156). Yuji, a former fishmonger who now owns Japanese restaurants in New York, Tokyo, and Bangkok, was kind enough to share his cheese sauce recipe for his mazemen. I love the combination of the creamy cheese, the subtle sweetness from the soy sauce, and the surprising brightness from the lemon zest. At his restaurant, he uses house-cured salmon as a topping. I've changed it up with thin slices of prosciutto for just a bit of saltiness. You could also replace the prosciutto with sautéed mushrooms and asparagus. Because the cheese sauce is so rich, you'll want to keep the toppings quite simple.

Serves 4 to 6

4 ounces Camembert cheese, cut into 1-inch pieces

½ cup heavy cream

½ cup neutral oil, such as canola or grapeseed

1 scallion, thinly sliced

1 garlic clove, thinly sliced

20 ounces fresh ramen noodles (see Tip)

6 tablespoons Sweet Soy Sauce (page 158)

1 cup thinly sliced sugar snap peas (about 3½ ounces)

8 slices prosciutto (about 2 ounces), torn into bite-size pieces

Grated zest of 2 lemons (about 2 tablespoons)

Freshly ground black pepper

1. Bring a large pot of water to a boil.

2. In a medium saucepan, combine the Camembert and heavy cream. Bring to a simmer over medium heat and cook until the Camembert is completely melted, about 4 minutes. (You will have visible pieces of rind.)

3. Pour the mixture into a blender or food processor, and blend or process until smooth. (Alternatively, use an immersion blender.) If there are visible pieces of rind, strain the mixture through a fine-mesh sieve and discard the rind.

4. In a small skillet, combine the oil, scallion, and garlic. Cook over low heat until the garlic turns slightly golden, about 10 minutes. Remove the skillet from the heat and set aside.

5. Add the noodles to the boiling water and cook according to the package directions. Reserving 1 cup of the cooking water, drain the noodles and transfer them to a large bowl. Immediately add the scallion oil and toss to coat. Add the cheese sauce and sweet soy sauce. Mix to coat evenly. If the cheese sauce isn't melting and coating the noodles, transfer everything to a large skillet and gently heat over low heat until the sauce coats the noodles, stirring in some of the reserved water to loosen up the sauce as needed.

6. Divide among four bowls and top with the sugar snap peas, prosciutto, and lemon zest. Season to taste with pepper and serve immediately.

tips | You can make the scallion oil, cheese sauce, and sweet soy sauce ahead of time. The scallion oil can be refrigerated in an airtight container for up to 1 week. The cheese sauce can be refrigerated in an airtight container for up to 3 days. Gently reheat the sauces before using.

• If you can't find ramen noodles, use the Spaghetti Baking Soda Hack (page 155).

Soba Noodle Salad
with Tahini Dressing
そばサラダ

I only started eating soba noodle salad when I moved to the States and started seeing it on restaurant menus or prepackaged at natural foods stores. It was eye-opening to see a Japanese ingredient being used in a nontraditional way. I soon started making soba salads as a quick lunch for restaurant family meals when I worked as a line cook. This refreshing and filling salad is perfect for the summer. The sauce lightly coats the noodles, but has a creamy, luscious consistency. It's nutty and a little sweet. You could even use this sauce as a salad dressing. Most soba noodles are made with a blend of buckwheat and wheat flour, but some are 100% buckwheat and are therefore gluten-free. Just make sure to check the ingredient list on the package.

Serves 4

TAHINI DRESSING

3 tablespoons tahini

2 tablespoons rice vinegar

2 tablespoons toasted sesame oil

2 teaspoons soy sauce

1 teaspoon sugar

1 tablespoon toasted white sesame seeds

Kosher salt

tips | When you're making the dressing, sometimes the tahini can seize up. If this happens, add water 1 teaspoon at a time, whisking, until the dressing is smooth.

SOBA NOODLE SALAD

9½ ounces (3 bundles) soba noodles

Kosher salt

1 Persian (mini) cucumber, cut into thin matchsticks

3 radishes, thinly sliced (about ½ cup)

2 cups baby spring mix (about 2 ounces)

1 bunch cilantro, leaves picked

• Toss the noodles with the dressing right before serving, otherwise the noodles will absorb too much dressing and become soggy.

1. Bring a large pot of water to a boil.

2. MAKE THE TAHINI DRESSING: In a large bowl, combine the tahini, rice vinegar, sesame oil, soy sauce, and sugar and mix well. Gradually add 1 tablespoon water, mixing well to combine. Add more water if the consistency is too thick. The dressing should be runny but a bit thicker than heavy cream. Add the sesame seeds and season with salt. The tahini dressing will keep in an airtight container in the refrigerator for up to 1 week.

3. MAKE THE SOBA NOODLE SALAD: Add the soba noodles to the pot of boiling water and cook according to the package directions. Drain and rinse under cold water. Transfer the noodles to the bowl of tahini dressing and toss to combine. Taste and season with salt, if desired.

4. Transfer the noodles to a large serving bowl or platter. Top with the cucumber, radishes, baby spring mix, and cilantro leaves.

Hiyashi Chuka

冷やし中華

We have a tradition in Japan of eating cold noodles during the summer months. Because it gets so hot and humid, we prefer chilled dishes to naturally cool ourselves down. I know it's the beginning of summer when restaurants start putting hiyashi chuka on their menu. I recommend making this dish during peak tomato season for the ripest, sweetest heirloom tomatoes.

Serves 4

SAUCE

¼ cup rice vinegar

¼ cup soy sauce

1 tablespoon mirin

½ tablespoon sugar

¼ cup toasted sesame oil

1 tablespoon fresh lemon juice

NOODLES

Kosher salt

20 ounces fresh ramen noodles (see Spaghetti Baking Soda Hack, page 155)

TOPPINGS

3 large eggs

2 teaspoons sugar

Pinch of kosher salt

1 tablespoon neutral oil, such as canola or grapeseed

1 hothouse cucumber or 2 Persian (mini) cucumbers

4 slices ham (about 2 ounces)

1 heirloom tomato, cut into wedges

2 tablespoons toasted white sesame seeds, coarsely ground (see Tip, page 41)

1. MAKE THE SAUCE: In a small saucepan, combine the rice vinegar, soy sauce, mirin, and sugar. Bring to a boil over high heat, stirring to dissolve the sugar and evaporate the alcohol. Remove the pan from the heat. Add ½ cup water, the sesame oil, and lemon juice. Let cool to room temperature and refrigerate until ready to use. The sauce will keep in an airtight container in the refrigerator for up to 2 weeks.

2. COOK THE NOODLES: Bring a large pot of salted water to a boil. Add the ramen and cook according to the package directions. Drain and rinse under cold water. Shake the sieve to remove excess water. Set aside. (If the noodles stick together, just rinse again and drain.)

3. MAKE THE TOPPINGS: In a bowl, whisk the eggs with the sugar and salt. In a medium nonstick skillet, heat the oil over medium-low heat. Wipe the excess oil with a paper towel. Add the egg mixture and cook until the eggs begin to set, 1 to 2 minutes. Using a spatula, flip the omelet and cook on the other side until set, about 1 minute more. Transfer to a cutting board and let cool. Once cool enough to touch, roll up the omelet and cut it crosswise into thin strips.

4. Thinly slice the cucumber(s) on a diagonal. Stack the slices and cut lengthwise into thin matchsticks. Roll up the ham and thinly slice crosswise.

5. Divide the ramen among four bowls and arrange the omelet, cucumber, ham, and tomato on top. Pour the sauce over the noodles and sprinkle with the ground sesame seeds.

gatherings

Butter and Pecan Stuffed Dates

デーツ&バター

Whenever I return to Japan and visit Tokyo, I stop by Higashiya, a wagashi store (traditional Japanese confectionery store), to buy their delicious dates stuffed with cultured butter and topped with walnuts. It's a simple treat, but the sweetness from the dates pairs beautifully with the richness of the butter, and the walnuts add a nice crunch. In wanting to re-create these dates, I came to the conclusion that for something this simple, you have to use high-quality ingredients. Medjool dates, which are soft and jammy, are a must. And for the butter, I prefer to use cultured European-style butter, which you can find at most higher-end grocery stores. I find that walnuts have a slight bitterness, so I've replaced them with pecans. These are perfect for serving as a dessert or passing around as an hors d'oeuvre before a meal.

Makes 12

12 pecan halves

12 Medjool dates

4 tablespoons (½ stick) unsalted butter, preferably cultured European butter, at room temperature

Flaky sea salt, such as Maldon, for sprinkling

tips | For a lighter version, you can substitute mascarpone cheese for the butter.

• If you have salted cultured butter, use it and omit the sea salt.

1. Preheat the oven to 350°F.

2. Spread the pecans in a single layer on a sheet pan. Toast, stirring halfway through, until golden and fragrant, 5 to 7 minutes. Let cool to room temperature.

3. Using a sharp knife, slit the dates lengthwise and remove the pits, being careful not to cut them in half.

4. Fill each date with about 1 teaspoon of the butter. Sprinkle with the salt. Top each date with a pecan half.

Edamame and Pistachio Dip

枝豆とピスタチオのディップ

I love preparing this appetizer for dinner parties or potlucks. It's incredibly easy and has a wonderful brightness from the lemon and parsley. Dips are much more popular in the US than in Japan, so I only started making this recipe when I moved here. The edamame and pistachios blend together to create a creamy, bright green dip. You can serve it with pita chips, crackers, and crudités, such as radishes, carrots, and cucumbers. It's delicious paired with the Miso Bagna Càuda (opposite) to make an appetizer spread.

Serves 6 to 8

1 cup shelled pistachios (about 4 ounces)

¼ cup extra-virgin olive oil, plus more for drizzling

1 cup frozen shelled edamame (about 4 ounces), thawed

Juice of 1 lemon (about 2 tablespoons)

1 garlic clove, finely grated

⅓ cup fresh parsley leaves, finely chopped

1. Preheat the oven to 350°F.

2. Spread the pistachios on a sheet pan. Toast in the oven until pale golden and fragrant, about 5 minutes. Let cool to room temperature.

3. In a food processor, pulse the pistachios until finely ground. Measure out 1 tablespoon ground pistachios and set aside for garnish. To the food processor, add ¼ cup water, the olive oil, edamame, lemon juice, and garlic. Process until a smooth paste forms. Add a little more water if the paste is too thick; it should be the consistency of miso.

4. Transfer the dip to a medium bowl and add the parsley. Using a rubber spatula, stir to combine. The dip will keep in an airtight container in the refrigerator for up to 3 days.

5. When ready to serve, transfer to a serving bowl. Drizzle with more olive oil and sprinkle with the reserved pistachios.

Miso Bagna Càuda

みそバーニャカウダ

Bagna càuda is a flavorful Italian dipping sauce made with anchovies and garlic. I replaced the anchovies with miso for a vegetarian-friendly, Japanese-inspired sauce. The saltiness of the miso is balanced by the richness of the butter and oil. Serve it with a beautiful array of fresh, crunchy vegetables either as an appetizer alongside the Edamame and Pistachio Dip (opposite) or on its own. The miso bagna càuda can be made ahead—just gently rewarm over low heat before serving, since the butter solidifies as it cools down. To make the bagna càuda vegan, replace the butter with the same amount of extra-virgin olive oil.

Serves 6 to 8

⅓ cup extra-virgin olive oil

8 garlic cloves, finely chopped or grated

3 tablespoons unsalted butter

2 tablespoons miso

1. In a small saucepan, combine the olive oil and garlic. Cook over low heat, stirring occasionally, until the garlic is fragrant and pale golden, about 10 minutes. Remove the pan from the heat.

2. Add the butter to the pan and stir until completely melted. Add the miso and whisk to dissolve. The miso will separate from the oil and butter; this is fine.

3. Serve warm. The miso bagna càuda will keep in an airtight container in the refrigerator for up to 3 days.

Mini Okonomiyaki

お好み焼き

Okonomiyaki is a savory pancake filled with cabbage and scallions and various toppings such as thinly sliced pork, seafood, and cheese. There are roughly two types of okonomiyaki: Osaka-style and Hiroshima-style, which is from my hometown. The Hiroshima-style is layered with noodles, and the Osaka-style has all the chopped ingredients mixed in with the batter. Even though I grew up in Hiroshima, I cook Osaka-style okonomiyaki at home because they're much easier to make. Yamaimo (mountain yam) is often used to make Osaka-style okonomiyaki fluffy, but it's hard to find in the US, so I use zucchini for a similar texture.

I rarely make okonomiyaki in Japan because they're so easy to find in restaurants. Usually, there's a table with a hot plate built into it for keeping the okonomiyaki hot while you eat it. Or sometimes you sit at the counter and the chef prepares it right in front of you. My close friend Susan Vu, who is an extraordinary recipe developer and food stylist and has tested many of the recipes for this book, came up with the brilliant idea of making mini okonomiyaki. They're much easier to cook and flip and can be served as a starter for a dinner party. When you add the bonito flakes to the piping-hot okonomiyaki, notice how they start "dancing" and moving to the steam.

Makes about 36 (serves 8 to 10 as an appetizer)

½ cup awase or kombu dashi, instant or homemade (see page 32), chilled

½ cup (65g) all-purpose flour

½ teaspoon baking powder

½ teaspoon kosher salt

1 zucchini, roughly chopped

½ head green cabbage, cut into about ½-inch pieces (about 3 cups)

3 scallions, thinly sliced

4 ounces jumbo (21/25) shrimp, peeled and deveined, cut into 1-inch pieces

2 large eggs

Neutral oil, such as canola or grapeseed

FOR SERVING

Okonomiyaki sauce

Kewpie mayonnaise

Sriracha (optional)

Bonito flakes

1. Place the dashi in a medium bowl. Gradually add the flour, whisking to combine. Add the baking powder and salt, whisking to combine until smooth.

2. In a food processor, pulse the zucchini until finely chopped. (Alternatively, grate the whole zucchini on the large holes of a box grater.) Transfer the zucchini to your largest bowl and add the cabbage, scallions, and shrimp. Stir in the flour-dashi mixture. Add the eggs, one at a time, mixing with a large spoon or chopsticks to incorporate. Refrigerate the batter for at least 30 minutes and up to 24 hours. (This will ensure a tender pancake.) When ready to cook, stir the batter again.

3. Preheat the oven to 250°F.

(recipe continues)

4. In a large nonstick skillet or cast-iron pan with a lid, heat 1 tablespoon oil over medium heat. Using a large spoon or measuring cup, scoop ¼ cup of the batter into the pan and spread it into a disk about 2½ inches in diameter and ½ inch thick. Depending on the size of your skillet, you can cook 4 to 6 (or more) at a time. Cook for 2 minutes. If the batter starts to spread, use a silicone spatula to push it back into a disk shape. Cover with a lid and cook until the bottom is lightly browned, 3 to 5 minutes more.

5. Flip the pancakes. Cover and cook for 3 minutes more. Uncover and cook until the bottom is crisp and browned, 2 to 4 minutes more. Transfer the okonomiyaki to a baking sheet and keep warm in the oven while you cook the remaining batter. Add more oil to the skillet as needed, about 1½ teaspoons per batch.

6. TO SERVE: Transfer the okonomiyaki to a serving platter or large plate. Drizzle with the okonomiyaki sauce, mayonnaise, and sriracha (if using). Top with a small handful of bonito flakes. Serve immediately. Okonomiyaki will keep wrapped in plastic and frozen for up to 1 month. To reheat, bake in a 375°F oven for 15 minutes.

tips | Okonomiyaki sauce is a specialty sauce that can be found at any Japanese grocery store. It's sweet and tangy and reminds me a bit of barbecue sauce.

• You can play around with the toppings. I like to dust the okonomiyaki with aonori (ground nori flakes), which you can find at Japanese grocery stores. Or finely cut nori seaweed sheets with scissors directly onto the pancakes.

Gyoza with Crispy Wings

羽根つき餃子

This gyoza recipe is from my mom, although she never measured the ingredients, so I had to guess the amounts from memory. It's one of the first dishes she taught me to make. The secret to a flavorful filling is using a lot of nira chives (see Tip). As a child, I remember being impressed by how quickly my mom folded the gyoza. By the time I'd make one gyoza, she had already made five.

One of my favorite ways to eat gyoza is by throwing a gyoza-making party. Wrapping the dumplings seems intimidating at first, but it's not that difficult. For the prettiest pleats, make sure to not overfill the gyoza. There are many ways to cook them, such as pan-frying, but I prefer this method of steam-frying in a cornstarch slurry. It forms a lacy, crispy crust on the bottom called "wings," or hane in Japanese.

Makes about 36 gyoza
(serves 6 to 8)

DIPPING SAUCE

¼ cup soy sauce

¼ cup rice vinegar

1 tablespoon toasted sesame oil

1 teaspoon chili oil

FILLING

8 ounces ground pork

1 cup finely chopped green cabbage (about 3 ounces)

¾ cup (about 1½ ounces) finely chopped nira chives (see Tip)

¼ cup finely chopped fresh shiitake mushrooms (about ¾ ounce)

½ teaspoon finely grated fresh ginger

1½ teaspoons soy sauce

1½ teaspoons toasted sesame oil

1½ teaspoons sake

½ teaspoon kosher salt

½ teaspoon freshly ground black pepper

DUMPLINGS

Cornstarch or potato starch

36 to 40 gyoza wrappers

Neutral oil, such as canola or grapeseed

Kosher salt

Toasted sesame oil

1. MAKE THE DIPPING SAUCE: In a small bowl, whisk together the soy sauce, rice vinegar, sesame oil, and chili oil. The sauce will keep in an airtight container in the refrigerator for up to 3 weeks.

2. MAKE THE FILLING: In a large bowl, combine the ground pork, cabbage, nira chives, shiitake, ginger, soy sauce, sesame oil, sake, salt, and pepper. Using your hands, mix well to combine.

3. MAKE THE DUMPLINGS: Dust a baking sheet with cornstarch. Fill a small bowl with water. Place a gyoza wrapper in the palm of your nondominant hand. Using your dominant hand, place a scant 1 tablespoon filling in the center of the wrapper. Dip your fingers in water and lightly wet one half of the wrapper's rim. Fold the wrapper in half. Using your fingertips, pleat only the top half of the wrapper, pressing against the bottom half to seal the gyoza (the bottom half of the wrapper remains flat; you only pleat one side of the wrapper). Place the gyoza on the prepared baking sheet. Repeat with the remaining wrappers and filling. Sprinkle with more cornstarch if the gyoza seem to be sticking together.

(recipe continues)

Uncooked gyoza will keep in the freezer in a resealable plastic freezer bag for up to 3 months.

4. In a 10-inch nonstick skillet with a lid, heat 2 teaspoons neutral oil over medium heat. Add enough gyoza to fit in a single layer (about 12 gyoza), arranging them in a circular pattern. Cook until slightly golden on the bottoms, 1 to 3 minutes.

5. In a small bowl or measuring cup, combine ⅓ cup water, 1½ teaspoons cornstarch, and a pinch of salt. Pour the cornstarch mixture into the skillet. Cover with a lid and steam the gyoza until most of the water has evaporated, 6 to 8 minutes. Uncover and continue cooking until the water has completely evaporated and the cornstarch has thickened to a gel-like web at the bottom of the skillet, about 2 minutes.

6. Drizzle some sesame oil around the edges of the gyoza. Increase the heat to medium-high and cook, uncovered, until the cornstarch dissolves and dries, forming "wings" that are lacy and crispy, 2 to 4 minutes. Remove the skillet from the heat and let the gyoza rest in the skillet until any bubbling subsides, 1 to 2 minutes.

7. Using chopsticks or a spatula, loosen the "wings." Place a large plate on top of the gyoza. Flip the skillet upside down to invert the gyoza onto the plate. Wipe the skillet clean and repeat with the remaining gyoza. Serve hot with the dipping sauce.

tip | This recipe calls for nira chives, also known as garlic chives or Chinese chives. They have a garlicky and more pungent flavor than regular chives, and I highly recommend going to a Japanese or Asian market for them. Alternatively, you can use the same amount of scallions or chives, though the flavor will be much milder, so be sure to add 2 grated garlic cloves to the filling, too.

Potato and Mushroom Gratin

じゃがいもときのこのグラタン

My mother would always make gratin in individual gratin dishes. The ovens in Japan are smaller than they are in the US, and most of them can't accommodate large casseroles. She would finish the gratin in the toaster oven, just to melt the cheese and crisp up the panko. I often make gratin in the winter, when the cold weather makes me crave the creamy béchamel sauce and soft layers of potatoes. Gratin is a very popular "yoshoku" dish—a Western-style recipe with a Japanese twist. It's inspired by French potato gratin. You can switch up the ingredients to suit your preference; sometimes I'll add shrimp, scallops, or bacon, or replace the potatoes with kabocha.

This gratin is perfect as a side for a Thanksgiving meal or a potluck. You can assemble it up to one day in advance, cover it tightly, refrigerate, and bake just before serving. Or you can serve it as a vegetarian main with the Green Salad with Umeboshi Dressing (page 57).

Serves 6 as a side

FILLING

1 tablespoon neutral oil, such as canola or grapeseed

1 white onion, thinly sliced (about 2 cups)

2 russet potatoes (about 1 pound), peeled and sliced 1/8 inch thick

6 ounces cremini mushrooms, sliced (about 2 cups)

BÉCHAMEL SAUCE

4 tablespoons (1/2 stick) unsalted butter

1/4 cup all-purpose flour

3 cups whole milk, at room temperature

3 tablespoons miso

TOPPINGS

1 cup shredded mozzarella cheese (about 4 ounces)

1/4 cup grated Parmesan cheese (about 1 ounce)

1/4 cup panko bread crumbs

Coarsely chopped fresh parsley leaves, for garnish

tip | Make sure the milk is at room temperature; otherwise, the béchamel might curdle.

1. Preheat the oven to 350°F.

2. MAKE THE FILLING: In a large skillet, heat the oil over medium heat. Add the onion and cook, stirring, until translucent, about 10 minutes. Add the potatoes and cook, stirring, until the edges are slightly translucent, about 5 minutes. Add the mushrooms and cook, stirring, until softened, 2 to 3 minutes. Transfer the mixture to a 2-quart baking dish (about 8 × 10 inches) and set aside.

3. MAKE THE BÉCHAMEL SAUCE: In a medium saucepan, melt the butter over medium heat. Sprinkle the flour over the butter. Cook, whisking, until bubbling, 2 to 3 minutes. While whisking constantly, slowly pour in the milk. Whisk in the miso and bring to a boil; this can take up to 25 minutes. Reduce the heat to medium-low and simmer, stirring often, until the sauce thickens, 10 to 15 minutes. Pour the béchamel over the potatoes.

4. TOP THE GRATIN: Sprinkle with the mozzarella, Parmesan, and panko. Cover with foil and bake, rotating the baking dish front to back halfway through, for 45 minutes. Remove the foil and bake until the top is golden brown, 15 to 20 minutes. Garnish with parsley.

Miso-Yogurt Roasted Chicken

丸鶏の味噌ヨーグルト漬け焼き

Roast chicken is a low-effort dish that always looks impressive. It's become one of my go-to dishes when I'm hosting a dinner for friends. Here I've spatchcocked the chicken (you remove the backbone so the chicken lies flat) so that it cooks more quickly and evenly. Marinating overnight with yogurt tenderizes the chicken and helps it stay juicy while also mellowing out the saltiness of miso, which gently flavors the meat. The sugar from the yogurt and miso also helps the chicken skin caramelize in the oven, turning it into a wonderfully crisp layer. The chili oil is optional but provides a welcome kick if you enjoy some heat. Or you could try scallion-lemon oil (see page 105) if you prefer no spice.

Serves 4 to 6

½ cup plain whole-milk Greek yogurt

¼ cup miso

3 garlic cloves, finely grated

1 whole chicken (about 3½ pounds)

Kosher salt and freshly ground black pepper

1½ pounds baby or fingerling potatoes, halved if large

2 tablespoons extra-virgin olive oil

Scallion-Garlic Chili Oil (optional; recipe follows)

Lemon wedges, for serving (optional)

1. In a small bowl, combine the yogurt, miso, and garlic. Stir well to combine and set aside.

2. Remove the giblets from the chicken and trim the excess fat around the cavity and neck. Using kitchen shears, cut along both sides of the backbone and remove it. Flip the chicken (breast-side up) and spread the thighs. Using your hand, push firmly between the breasts to flatten. Pat the chicken dry with a paper towel. Place the chicken in a large container and generously season it with salt and pepper. Smear the yogurt-miso mixture all over the chicken. Cover with plastic wrap and refrigerate overnight.

3. Remove the plastic wrap and scrape the yogurt marinade from the chicken. Let the chicken sit at room temperature for 1 hour.

4. Preheat the oven to 400°F with a rack in the lower third.

5. In a large bowl, combine the potatoes and olive oil and mix to coat. Season with salt and pepper. Place the potatoes on a sheet pan or roasting pan. Place the chicken, breast-side up, on top of the potatoes, making sure the chicken is not directly touching the baking sheet.

6. Roast, rotating the baking sheet front to back every 20 minutes, until a meat thermometer inserted into the thickest part of the breast registers 165°F, 45 minutes to 1 hour. If the chicken is browning too much at the 30-minute mark, cover it with foil and continue roasting until cooked through. If the potatoes aren't tender when the chicken is done, return them to the oven and continue roasting until they can be easily pierced with a fork.

7. Let the chicken rest for 10 minutes. Serve with the chili oil and lemon wedges, if desired.

(recipe continues)

Scallion-Garlic Chili Oil

Makes about ⅔ cup

2 tablespoons crushed red pepper flakes

5 garlic cloves, thinly sliced

1 scallion, thinly sliced

1 teaspoon onion powder

⅓ cup neutral oil, such as canola or grapeseed

¼ cup toasted sesame oil

½ tablespoon white sesame seeds

1 teaspoon sugar

1 teaspoon kosher salt

1. In a small saucepan, combine the pepper flakes, garlic, scallion, and onion powder. Add the neutral oil and set aside for 30 minutes.

2. Set the pan over low heat and cook, stirring, until the garlic is golden, 20 to 25 minutes, being careful not to brown the garlic and scallions. Add the sesame oil, sesame seeds, sugar, and salt. Stir well to dissolve the sugar and salt. Remove the pot from the heat. Let cool completely and transfer to a glass jar or an airtight container. The chili oil will keep in an airtight container in the refrigerator for up to 1 month.

Easy Sushi Balls

簡単手まり寿司

Temari is an embroidered colorful handball, often made with cotton and silk threads or pieces of fabric. We call these sushi balls temari sushi because they resemble the handballs: They're bite-size rice balls covered with colorful toppings, such as thinly sliced raw fish. We often serve them at parties and celebrations. They're cute and incredibly easy to make. I've started making temari sushi using store-bought cured meats and fish, such as prosciutto and smoked salmon. Because the meat and fish are already thinly sliced, they are perfect for covering a small ball of rice. Plus, since they are already salty, you don't need to dip the balls in soy sauce.

Makes about 15 sushi balls each

tip | Select basil sprigs with smaller leaves, as those tend to be better for garnishing. If the basil leaf is too big, simply tear or cut it in half.

Prosciutto and Basil Sushi Balls

生ハムとバジルの手まり寿司

4 to 5 slices prosciutto

15 fresh basil leaves

2 cups freshly cooked Sushi Rice (page 119)

1. Cut or tear the prosciutto into about 2 × 1-inch rectangles. No need to be too precise.

2. Cut a piece of plastic wrap that is about 5 × 12 inches. Place one piece of prosciutto in the center of the plastic wrap, followed by one basil leaf and 1 heaping tablespoon of the rice. Using the plastic wrap, wrap the rice around the filling and tightly twist the plastic at the top to make a ball.

3. Unwrap the rice ball and place it on a platter or large plate. Repeat with the remaining ingredients, using the same piece of plastic wrap.

(recipe continues)

Smoked Salmon and Cucumber Sushi Balls

スモークサーモンときゅうりの手まり寿司

4 to 5 slices smoked salmon

1 Persian (mini) cucumber, very thinly sliced

2 cups freshly cooked Sushi Rice (page 119)

Fresh dill, for garnish

1. Cut or tear the smoked salmon into about 2 × 1-inch rectangles. No need to be too precise.

2. Cut a piece of plastic wrap that is about 5 × 12 inches. Place a piece of smoked salmon in the center of the plastic wrap, followed by 2 slices of cucumber and 1 heaping tablespoon of the rice. Using the plastic wrap, wrap the rice around the filling and tightly twist the plastic at the top to make a ball.

3. Unwrap the rice ball and transfer to a platter or large plate. Repeat with the remaining ingredients, using the same piece of plastic wrap. Top each sushi ball with a sprig of dill.

Roast Beef Sushi Balls

ローストビーフの手まり寿司

4 to 5 thin slices roast beef

2 cups freshly cooked Sushi Rice (page 119)

1 tablespoon soy sauce

Wasabi paste, for topping

1. Cut the roast beef slices into about 4 × 2-inch strips. No need to be too precise.

2. Cut a piece of plastic wrap that is about 5 × 12 inches. Place 1 heaping tablespoon of the rice in the center of the plastic wrap. Using the plastic wrap, wrap the rice and twist the plastic tightly to make a ball. Remove the plastic wrap.

3. Place 2 strips of roast beef crosswise over the rice ball, wrapping it around to completely cover the rice. Return the sushi ball to the plastic and wrap it around the ball, twisting tightly so that the roast beef adheres to the rice. Unwrap the rice ball and transfer it to a platter or large plate. Repeat with the remaining ingredients, using the same piece of plastic wrap.

4. Brush each ball with a little soy sauce and dot with a small amount of wasabi.

Chirashizushi

ちらし寿司

Chirashi means "scattered" in Japanese, referring to the way fish is scattered over rice in this sushi dish. It's one of the most common ways to make sushi at home and is perfect for when you want to impress guests without spending hours in the kitchen. Presented on a large platter and with colorful toppings, it makes for a gorgeous, festive centerpiece. We often make chirashi for celebrations, such as birthdays, graduations, or Hinamatsuri (Girls' Day, also known as Doll Festival) on March 3. Since this recipe requires sushi-grade fish, which can be hard to find, I recommend saving it for a special occasion. In my version, I've marinated the fish in a flavorful sauce. I like how the marinade changes the texture of the fish, so it has a bit of chew.

Serves 6 to 8

FISH

¼ cup mirin

¼ cup soy sauce

1 pound sushi-grade tuna, such as ahi tuna or bluefin tuna, cut into ½-inch cubes

1 pound sushi-grade salmon, cut into ½-inch cubes

RICE AND TOPPINGS

2 tablespoons toasted white sesame seeds

4 cups freshly cooked Sushi Rice (page 119)

1 English cucumber or 2 Persian (mini) cucumbers

½ teaspoon kosher salt

1 Tamagoyaki (page 84), cut into 1-inch cubes

1 avocado, cut into 1-inch cubes

3 radishes (optional), thinly sliced

2 ounces salmon roe (optional)

Soy sauce, for serving

tips | First, get the rice started on the stove or in an electric rice cooker. Then marinate the fish. While the fish is marinating, make the tamagoyaki (rolled omelet) and prepare the other toppings. This way, all the components are ready to be assembled in the last step.

• I usually serve the soy sauce in a small milk pitcher so that each person can add the amount they like.

1. **PREPARE THE FISH:** In a small saucepan, bring the mirin to a simmer over medium-high heat and cook for 2 minutes to evaporate the alcohol. Let cool to room temperature and add the soy sauce.

2. In a medium bowl, combine the tuna and salmon. Add the mirin–soy sauce mixture and mix to coat the fish. Cover with plastic wrap and refrigerate for 30 minutes.

3. **MEANWHILE, PREPARE THE RICE AND TOPPINGS:** Sprinkle the sesame seeds over the sushi rice and mix to evenly distribute. Trim the ends from the cucumber, then halve lengthwise. Cut each half lengthwise into three strips, then cut crosswise into ½-inch pieces. Put the cucumber in a sieve and sprinkle with the salt. Mix well and set aside for 15 minutes to drain. Using your hands and paper towels, squeeze out any excess water. Set aside.

4. Spread the sushi rice in the bottom of a large serving bowl. Drain the marinated fish and discard the marinade. Scatter the fish evenly over the rice. Fill in the gaps with the omelet cubes, avocado, and cucumber. Top with the radishes and salmon roe, if using. Serve with soy sauce.

Chicken Hot Pot with Ponzu

鶏の水炊き

My family often cooked hot pots in the wintertime, and when I was a college student, it was a favorite dinner-party meal. We would gather around a table with the hot pot at the center and continue adding ingredients to the simmering broth until we were full. If you have a portable gas burner or induction heater, you can cook the chicken meatballs and thighs in the kitchen and finish the vegetables and mushrooms at the table; otherwise use a donabe (Japanese clay pot) or Dutch oven, as they retain heat. When I moved to the US, I continued to cook and eat hot pots. One friend would throw a "hot pot party" for New Year's Eve, and it became a tradition we all looked forward to.

Serves 4 to 6

KOMBU DASHI

1 (4-inch) square piece kombu

CHICKEN MEATBALLS

1 pound ground chicken

½ teaspoon kosher salt

1 large egg

1 tablespoon sake

1 teaspoon soy sauce

2 scallions, finely chopped

1 teaspoon finely grated fresh ginger

2 tablespoons cornstarch or potato starch

HOT POT

1 pound boneless, skinless chicken thighs, cut into 1 inch-pieces

1 carrot, sliced on a diagonal ¼ inch thick (about 1 cup)

2 leeks, white parts only, thinly sliced on a diagonal (about 3 cups)

¼ head napa cabbage, cut into 2-inch pieces (about 2 cups), white stems and leafy greens separated

14 ounces medium-firm tofu, halved and sliced ½ inch thick

8 shiitake or baby bella mushrooms, halved

5 ounces enoki or oyster mushrooms

DIPPING SAUCE

2 cups ponzu, store-bought or homemade (recipe follows)

4 scallions (optional), thinly sliced

Shichimi togarashi (optional)

Yuzu kosho (optional; see Tip)

tips | You can add cooked rice to the pot to make zōsui (rice porridge). Or add cooked udon noodles to bulk up the meal. Just make sure to add the rice or noodles in the last step, just before serving.

• Yuzu kosho is a spicy fermented paste made with chiles, yuzu, and salt. Make sure to taste it before adding it to the hot pot—you'll probably only use a little, depending on your heat preference. You can find it online or at Japanese grocery stores.

• Don't skip the ponzu dipping sauce. If you don't have time to make your own ponzu, you can find it at Asian or Japanese grocery stores, or maybe even your regular grocery store if you're lucky.

1. MAKE THE KOMBU DASHI: Place the kombu in a donabe (Japanese clay pot) or Dutch oven. Add 6 to 8 cups water. Adjust the water amount depending on the size of the pot you are using. For a donabe, the water should come two-thirds up the sides of the donabe. For a Dutch oven, fill it halfway with water. Soak the kombu for 30 minutes. Remove and discard the kombu.

2. MAKE THE CHICKEN MEATBALLS: In a medium bowl, combine the chicken and salt. Mix until the chicken is sticky and paste-like. Add the egg, sake, soy sauce, scallions, and ginger. Using your hands, mix well until fully combined. Add the cornstarch and mix well until combined. Refrigerate until ready to use.

3. SET UP THE HOT POT: Bring the kombu dashi to a simmer over medium-high heat. Using 2 small spoons, shape the meatball mixture into balls and drop them into the pot. Repeat until the meatballs fill one-third of the pot, about 12 meatballs or half of the meatball mixture. Add the chicken thighs. Cook until the meatballs and chicken thighs are cooked through, about 8 minutes. Using a spoon or a mesh skimmer, skim off any impurities that rise to the surface.

4. Reduce the heat to medium. Add about one-third of each ingredient to the pot in this order: carrot, leeks, white stems from the napa cabbage, tofu, and mushrooms. Place the ingredients in their own sections, so they remain separate. Do not overfill the pot. Cover and cook until all the ingredients are tender, about 5 minutes. Add the leafy greens from the napa cabbage and cover. Cook until wilted, about 3 minutes more.

5. MAKE THE DIPPING SAUCE: Place the ponzu in a bowl. If desired, add the scallions, shichimi togarashi, and/or yuzu kosho.

6. Place the hot pot at the center of the table with chopsticks or tongs for serving. Give everyone a small individual bowl of dipping sauce. Each person can serve themselves from the hot pot, choosing a little bit of everything to dip in the sauce.

7. Once there are no more ingredients in the pot, add the remaining uncooked ingredients (meatballs, tofu, mushrooms, vegetables) and cook following the directions in steps 3 and 4. Serve again.

(recipe continues)

Ponzu
ポン酢

Ponzu is usually made with yuzu, but yuzu is difficult to find in American grocery stores and is a seasonal ingredient. I use lemon instead for my ponzu. If you can find Meyer lemons, use those for a milder ponzu. This sauce can also be used as a dipping sauce for Gyoza with Crispy Wings (page 177).

Makes about 2 cups

¼ cup sake

¼ cup mirin

1 cup soy sauce

¼ cup rice vinegar

½ cup (4g) bonito flakes

⅔ cup fresh lemon juice or Meyer lemon juice

In a small saucepan, combine the sake and mirin. Cook over medium heat for 30 to 40 seconds to evaporate the alcohol. Remove the pan from the heat. Add the soy sauce, rice vinegar, bonito flakes, and lemon juice. Stir to combine. The ponzu will keep in an airtight container in the refrigerator for up to 1 month.

Inarizushi

いなり寿司

Inarizushi, or tofu-pouch sushi, is rice wrapped in a braised fried tofu pouch called aburaage. In Japan, we say it's the favorite food of shrine foxes, so you can think of this recipe as "fox sushi." For a vegan version, use the Kombu Dashi (page 32) to cook the aburaage. In Japan, we often buy ready-made inarizushi at convenience stores and grocery stores, or in bentos sold at train stations. But it's easy to make a big quantity at home, and it's the perfect sushi to bring to a picnic or potluck because it keeps at room temperature for several hours and is easily transportable. You can also add it to a bento (to replace rice) or serve it as an appetizer for a dinner party. As a child, inarizushi was my preferred sushi because it's a bit sweet (the tofu soaks up the delicious sweet-salty sauce) and can be eaten with your hands.

Makes 16 pieces

8 aburaage (fried tofu pouches)

1 cup awase or kombu dashi, instant or homemade (see page 32)

3 tablespoons soy sauce

1 tablespoon mirin

3 tablespoons sugar

1 tablespoon toasted black sesame seeds (optional)

4 cups freshly cooked Sushi Rice (page 119)

1. Roll each aburaage with a chopstick, the way you would use a rolling pin, so it is easier to open. If the aburaage is shaped like a square, cut it in half on a diagonal to make two triangle pouches. If the aburaage is a rectangle, cut in half crosswise to make two square-like pouches.

2. Bring a medium pot of water to a boil. Add the aburaage and simmer until softened and collapsed, about 2 minutes. Remove from the pot and rinse in a fine-mesh sieve under cold running water. Once cool to the touch, squeeze out any liquid from the aburaage, being careful not to tear the pouch.

3. In a medium pot, arrange the aburaage in concentric circles, following the shape of the pot and overlapping to fit in one layer. Make a parchment cartouche (see page 23) that fits inside the pot and set aside.

4. In a small bowl, whisk the dashi, soy sauce, mirin, and sugar until the sugar is completely dissolved. Pour the sauce over the aburaage. Bring to a boil, then reduce the heat to medium-low and cover with the parchment cartouche. Simmer for 10 minutes, then remove the cartouche and discard. If there is still a lot of liquid, continue to cook, uncovered, until most of the liquid has reduced, about 5 minutes. (There should be a thin layer of liquid at the bottom of the pot.) Remove the pot from the heat. Flip the aburaage and let cool to room temperature in the remaining cooking liquid. Use your hands to squeeze the excess cooking liquid out of each aburaage and transfer them to a plate.

5. If using the sesame seeds, sprinkle them over the sushi rice and mix in to evenly distribute. Wet your hands with a little water to prevent the rice from sticking. Take about 2 tablespoons of the sushi rice and, using your hands, shape it into an oval. Fill the aburaage pouch with the rice. Repeat with the remaining aburaage. Serve immediately or refrigerate in an airtight container for up to 1 day.

Temaki Party

手巻き寿司

I love to throw a temaki (hand roll) party for friends. It's not too much work once the guests arrive, as all the ingredients can be prepared in advance, and it's always a big hit for a gathering. Just make sure to cook the rice on the day of the party and keep it at room temperature. (Rice will harden when refrigerated.) I've listed ingredient suggestions below, but you don't have to make all of them, and you can add almost anything you like to a roll. I recommend asking your guests to bring some of the fillings, and even surprise you with what they choose. Last time, my friends brought kimchi and charcuterie. Thanks to them, I discovered that I love prosciutto cotto in my hand rolls. I also think this is a great way to introduce sushi to kids.

Serves 6

20 (7½ × 8-inch) sheets nori (seaweed)

8 cups freshly cooked Sushi Rice (page 119)

FILLINGS

Omelet (recipe follows)

Spicy Tuna (recipe follows)

Boilod Shrimp (recipe follows)

6 slices ham, halved lengthwise

2 avocadoes, thinly sliced

1 English cucumber, cut into 3-inch-long matchsticks

1 cup kimchi

2 ounces salmon roe

Mayonnaise, preferably Kewpie, for topping (optional)

Soy sauce, for serving

tips | I like to add Kewpie mayonnaise to shrimp and avocado hand rolls.

• Another filling I love is the flavorful pork topping from the Creamy Soy Milk Udon (page 159). Just make the recipe for the topping minus the bok choy.

Cut the nori into 4-inch squares. Add about 2 tablespoons of rice on one side of a nori square, spreading it into a thin layer. Place the desired fillings on the rice, add a squeeze of mayonnaise (if using), and roll up the nori to close. Dip into the soy sauce and eat with your hands.

Omelet

厚焼き玉子

4 large eggs

1 tablespoon sugar

Pinch of kosher salt

2 teaspoons neutral oil, such as
canola or grapeseed

1. In a small bowl, mix the eggs, sugar, and salt until
the yolks are blended with the whites.

2. In a small nonstick skillet or a tamagoyaki pan (see
page 25), heat the oil over medium heat. Add half
of the egg mixture and cook until the bottom is set,
about 3 minutes. Flip and cook on the other side
until set, about 1 minute. Transfer the omelet to a
plate. Repeat with the remaining egg mixture. You
will have two thin omelets.

3. Cut the omelets into 3 × ½-inch strips.

Spicy Tuna

スパイシーツナ

2 (5-ounce) cans tuna in olive oil,
drained

2 tablespoons mayonnaise, preferably
Kewpie

1 tablespoon sriracha

Kosher salt

In a small bowl, mix the tuna, mayonnaise, and
sriracha. Season to taste with salt.

Boiled Shrimp

ボイルえび

Kosher salt

½ pound jumbo (21/25) shrimp,
peeled and deveined

1. Bring a large pot of salted water to a boil. Add the
shrimp and cook until pink, about 2 minutes. Drain
the shrimp and transfer to a large plate. Refrigerate
until cold.

2. Using a sharp knife, cut the shrimp in half
horizontally.

sweets
& breads

Matcha Granola

抹茶のグラノラ

I only started making granola after I moved to the US, as our ovens in Japan are often too small for large baking sheets. I love this version that includes matcha. A powdered green tea, matcha contains some caffeine and gives you an extra kick at breakfast time. I've chosen to add the matcha after baking the granola to preserve its vibrant green color. You can eat the granola on its own as an afternoon snack or for breakfast with yogurt and fresh seasonal fruit. Sometimes I'll even serve it for dessert with a scoop of vanilla ice cream.

Makes about 5½ cups

3 cups rolled oats

1 cup raw pecan halves

1 cup unsweetened coconut chips

⅓ cup raw pumpkin seeds

1 teaspoon kosher salt

⅓ cup extra-virgin olive oil

2 tablespoons light brown sugar

⅓ cup maple syrup

1 tablespoon (6g) matcha powder

1 tablespoon toasted white sesame seeds

1. Preheat the oven to 300°F. Line a sheet pan with parchment paper.

2. In a large bowl, combine the oats, pecans, coconut chips, pumpkin seeds, and salt. Mix well and set aside.

3. In a small saucepan, combine the olive oil and brown sugar. Cook over medium-low heat, stirring, until the brown sugar is dissolved, 2 to 3 minutes. Remove the pot from the heat and stir in the maple syrup.

4. Drizzle the syrup mixture over the oat mixture. Using a flexible spatula, stir well to coat all the ingredients. Spread the granola in an even layer on the prepared pan.

5. Bake, stirring halfway through, until golden, 30 to 40 minutes.

6. Remove the pan from the oven and immediately sprinkle with the matcha and sesame seeds. Stir to combine. Let cool completely. The granola will keep in an airtight container at room temperature for up to 3 weeks.

Simple Strawberry Shortcake

苺のシートパン・ショートケーキ

Strawberry shortcake is one of the most popular cakes in Japan, especially for celebrations such as birthdays, graduations, and even Christmas. Growing up, I always requested one for my birthday. This is a simple version with one layer, which is easier to make and travels better than multilayer ones.

You can make the sponge cake up to 2 days in advance. Wrap it tightly with plastic and store it in the refrigerator, then bring it to room temperature before serving. The mascarpone whipped cream and the strawberries can be prepared up to 3 hours in advance. Just make sure to brush the cake with syrup and assemble right before serving.

Makes one 9 × 13-inch cake

SPONGE CAKE

Softened butter for the pan

¼ cup (60g) whole milk

5 tablespoons (70g) unsalted butter

6 large eggs, at room temperature

1 cup (200g) granulated sugar

1¾ cups (228g) all-purpose flour

SIMPLE SYRUP

¼ cup (50g) granulated sugar

1 tablespoon rum or brandy (optional)

TOPPING

10 to 12 strawberries (about 12 ounces)

1 cup (240g) heavy cream

8 ounces (226g) mascarpone cheese

2 tablespoons powdered sugar

1 teaspoon vanilla extract

1. MAKE THE SPONGE CAKE: Preheat the oven to 350°F. Line the bottom and sides of a 9 × 13-inch pan with parchment paper. The sides should be about 2 inches tall. Butter the parchment paper (no need to butter the sides).

2. In a small saucepan, combine the milk and butter. Warm over medium-low heat until the butter is melted. Set aside.

3. Fill a very large bowl one-third full with hot water to create a hot water bath. In a large bowl that fits inside the very large bowl, combine the eggs and granulated sugar. Place the large bowl inside the bowl with the hot water. This will help dissolve the sugar and speed up the process of whipping the eggs.

4. Using a handheld electric mixer, beat the egg mixture on high speed until pale yellow and thick, 10 to 15 minutes. The mixture should be warm to the touch, similar to your body temperature. When you lift the mixer, the ribbons should keep their shape for a few seconds before dissolving. Reduce the speed to low and beat for 3 minutes more. This will prevent large air pockets from forming in the cake. Remove the bowl from the water bath.

(recipe continues)

5. Sift half of the flour over the batter and, using a rubber spatula, fold in the flour until completely incorporated. Repeat with the remaining flour. There shouldn't be any visible streaks of flour.

6. Drizzle the milk-butter mixture over the batter. Using a rubber spatula, fold it into the batter until just incorporated. Pour the batter into the prepared pan. Tap the pan two to three times on the counter to remove any large air bubbles.

7. Reduce the oven temperature to 325°F and bake, rotating the pan front to back halfway through, until golden brown, 40 to 45 minutes. A toothpick or cake tester inserted into the middle should come out clean. Using oven mitts or a dish towel, hold the cake pan a few inches above a work surface or the stove and drop it onto the surface. (If using a ceramic dish, don't lift it too high.) This shocks the sponge and prevents it from shrinking. Drop the cake a second time. Let the cake cool completely in the pan.

8. Meanwhile, make the simple syrup: In a small saucepan, combine the granulated sugar and ¼ cup water. Bring to a boil over high heat, stirring until the sugar is dissolved. Remove the pan from the heat and add the rum, if desired. Set aside.

9. PREPARE THE TOPPING: Cut half of the strawberries lengthwise in half. If the strawberries are large, cut them into quarters.

10. In a medium bowl, combine the heavy cream, mascarpone, powdered sugar, and vanilla. Whisk until stiff peaks form. Refrigerate the mascarpone whipped cream until ready to use.

11. Using a pastry brush, brush the simple syrup onto the cake. Using a small offset spatula or a spoon, coat the top of the cake with the mascarpone whipped cream. Arrange the strawberries on top.

tips | You can soak cold eggs in warm water for a few minutes to bring them to room temperature.

• Make sure to warm up the egg mixture. Warm eggs trap air better when whisking. If the eggs are too cold, it'll be harder to incorporate air into the whipped eggs, and the cake won't rise as much.

• Once I add the flour, I like to use a rubber spatula to incorporate it instead of a whisk. This prevents overmixing, which would yield a denser cake.

Matcha Snacking Cake

抹茶ケーキ

This cake is not too sweet, so it's perfect as an everyday cake for snacking in the morning or afternoon. The recipe is incredibly easy and can be made entirely in one bowl. I use whole milk and Greek yogurt for an extra tender crumb. I always have both ingredients in the fridge and love this combination for baking cakes. You won't taste any tartness from the yogurt, it's there just for moisture. For a brighter green color, I recommend ceremonial matcha.

Makes one 9-inch cake

Neutral oil, for the pan

2 large eggs, at room temperature (see Tip, page 207)

1 cup (200g) sugar

½ cup (143g) plain whole-milk Greek yogurt, at room temperature

½ cup (120g) whole milk, at room temperature

½ cup (120g) neutral oil, such as canola or grapeseed

1 teaspoon vanilla extract

1¾ cups (228g) all-purpose flour

2 tablespoons (12g) matcha

1 teaspoon baking powder

½ teaspoon kosher salt

Whipped cream, for serving (optional; see Tip)

1. Preheat the oven to 300°F. Grease a 9-inch round cake pan with oil. Line the bottom of the pan with parchment paper.

2. In a large bowl, whisk the eggs and sugar until foamy. Add the yogurt, milk, oil, and vanilla and whisk to combine.

3. Sift in the flour, matcha, and baking powder. Add the salt. Whisk until smooth. Pour the batter into the prepared cake pan. Tap the pan against the counter to release any air bubbles. Place the pan on a baking sheet.

4. Bake, rotating the pan front to back halfway through, until a toothpick comes out clean, 40 to 45 minutes.

5. Transfer the cake to a wire rack and let cool completely before unmolding. Top with whipped cream, if desired. Leftover cake will keep in an airtight container in the refrigerator for up to 3 days or wrapped tightly in plastic and frozen for up to 1 month.

tips | Use the cartouche technique (see page 23) to make a parchment round for lining the cake pan.

• For a chocolate cake, substitute the same amount of cocoa powder for the matcha powder.

• If you have leftover Sweet Red Bean Paste (page 227), you can make a red bean–flavored whipped cream by folding in 2 tablespoons Sweet Red Bean Paste into 1 cup whipped cream.

Steamed Cakes

蒸しパン

Mushipan, or steamed cake, is a nostalgic treat that reminds me of my childhood. Whenever I came home from school in the afternoon, my mother would greet me with a snack, either store-bought or homemade. This was one of my favorites. I liked to eat the small cake while it was still warm, fresh from the steamer. The inside was barely sweet and subtly flavored with matcha, chocolate, or vanilla.

Steaming the cakes yields an incredibly moist crumb that you wouldn't achieve in the oven. I also love how the tops puff up into a dome. Anything round is cute, am I right?

Makes 6 cakes

Neutral oil, for the ramekins

4 large eggs, at room temperature (see Tip, page 207)

½ cup (100g) sugar

¼ cup (60g) neutral oil, such as canola or grapeseed

½ cup (120g) whole milk, at room temperature

2 tablespoons plain whole-milk Greek yogurt

1 teaspoon vanilla extract

2 cups (260g) all-purpose flour

2 teaspoons baking powder

4 teaspoons matcha powder or 2 tablespoons cocoa powder (optional)

1. Grease six 3½-inch (3½-ounce) ramekins with oil.

2. Pour 1 inch of water into a large pot set with a steamer. Wrap the underside of the lid with a kitchen towel to prevent condensation from dripping onto the cakes. Make sure to tie the ends of the towel over the top of the lid so the fabric doesn't catch on fire. Bring the water to a boil over high heat. (If you don't have a steamer, see Tip. If you are using a bamboo steamer, there's no need to wrap the lid with a kitchen towel.)

3. In a large bowl, whisk the eggs and sugar until pale yellow. Add the oil, milk, yogurt, and vanilla. Whisk until smooth and combined.

4. In a medium bowl, combine the flour and baking powder. Whisk in the matcha powder or cocoa powder, if using. Sift the flour mixture over the egg mixture. Using a rubber spatula, mix in the flour until just incorporated. (Be careful not to overmix the batter;

it's fine to have a few lumps.) Spoon the batter into the prepared ramekins, filling them two-thirds of the way up.

5. Once the water comes to a boil, reduce the heat to medium and bring to a simmer. Place the ramekins in the steamer and cover with the towel-wrapped lid. Cook until a cake tester or toothpick comes out clean, 15 to 20 minutes. Use tongs to carefully transfer the cakes to a wire rack and let cool for 5 minutes. Eat the cakes warm or at room temperature.

tip | If you don't have a steamer, you can use a large skillet or a pot with a lid. Pour ½ inch of water into the skillet. Take two pieces of paper towel and fold each one in half lengthwise. Line the bottom of the skillet with the folded paper towels. They will provide a cushion for the ramekins, so they don't rattle against the skillet. The cook time will be the same as when using a steamer.

Matcha Tiramisu

抹茶ティラミス

When I was a student in Osaka, I would often spend weekends in Kyoto, a city known for its delicious matcha, and I'd always treat myself to a matcha dessert. This recipe is inspired by a spectacular matcha tiramisu I ate there at a teahouse called Maccha House. The tiramisu was beautifully presented in individual masu cups (square wooden boxes used for sake), but what I loved most were the textures and flavors: it was so soft and creamy and balanced. The sweetness from the cream complemented the natural bitterness of matcha. I've re-created the smooth, airy cream along with a nice, strong matcha base. I like to make this dessert in the summer when I don't want to turn on my oven.

Serves 4 to 6

2 tablespoons (12g) plus 1½ teaspoons matcha powder

1 cup hot water

12 to 14 ladyfingers

2 large eggs, separated

6 tablespoons (75g) sugar

1 teaspoon rum or brandy

8 ounces (226g) mascarpone cheese, cold

1. Place 2 tablespoons of the matcha in a mug or small shallow bowl. Pour ¼ cup of the hot water into the mug. Using a small whisk or matcha whisk, whisk to dissolve the matcha. Add the remaining ¾ cup hot water. Working one at a time, dip the ladyfingers into the matcha, holding them for 5 seconds to soak. Layer them in a 9-inch round ceramic or glass baking dish. Set aside.

2. In a stand mixer fitted with the whisk (or in a bowl with a hand mixer), beat the egg whites until foamy. Set aside.

3. In a small saucepan, combine 3 tablespoons of the sugar and 2 tablespoons water. Bring to a boil over medium-high heat and cook until the sugar dissolves and thickens, being careful not to caramelize the sugar, about 5 minutes. If you have a thermometer, the sugar mixture should be between 245° and 248°F.

4. With the mixer on medium speed, drizzle the hot syrup into the egg whites. Whisk until stiff, glossy peaks form, about 5 minutes. Refrigerate until ready to use.

5. Pour 1 inch of water into a medium saucepan and bring to a gentle simmer over medium heat. In a heatproof medium bowl (that can sit over the saucepan without touching the water), whisk together the egg yolks, rum, and remaining 3 tablespoons sugar. Set the bowl over the saucepan and whisk the egg yolk mixture until pale yellow and doubled in volume, about 5 minutes. Remove the bowl from the saucepan and let cool for 5 minutes.

6. In a separate medium bowl, whisk the mascarpone cheese to loosen it. Slowly add the warmed egg yolk mixture to the mascarpone cheese. Whisk until smooth. Using a rubber spatula, fold in the whipped egg whites. Mix until smooth and just combined.

7. Pour the mascarpone mixture over the ladyfingers. Cover with plastic wrap and refrigerate for 1 hour and up to overnight.

8. Dust the top with the remaining 1½ teaspoons matcha before serving.

Almond "Tofu" Pudding

杏仁豆腐

Annin dōfu translates to "apricot kernel tofu" and is traditionally made with apricot kernels and agar-agar, a gelatin derived from seaweed. This simple and elegant dessert is originally from China and is extremely popular in Japan—you can find it at Chinese restaurants and convenience stores. It will remind you of tofu although it doesn't contain any soybeans. The store-bought version has the texture of a firm jelly, whereas mine is smooth, similar to a panna cotta. I was inspired by a friend who worked with me at Disney in Orlando. One day she brought a delicious annin dōfu to a dinner party. The soft texture was unlike anything else I'd eaten, so I asked for her secret: a combination of heavy cream and milk. She also added amaretto to the syrup for a lovely almond fragrance. (You can omit the liquor for an alcohol-free dessert.) Often the pudding is served with canned fruit, but I prefer garnishing with goji berries, as they add a pop of color without overpowering the subtle flavors.

Serves 4

PUDDING

1 envelope (7g) unflavored gelatin powder

1 cup (240g) whole milk

¾ cup (180g) heavy cream

3½ tablespoons (45g) sugar

½ teaspoon almond extract

SYRUP

½ cup (100g) sugar

1 tablespoon amaretto (optional)

Goji berries, for topping (optional)

1. MAKE THE PUDDING: Pour 1 tablespoon water into a small bowl. Sprinkle the gelatin over the water. Wait for 1 minute, then add another 1 tablespoon water to cover any dry spots. Set aside to bloom for 5 minutes.

2. In a small saucepan, combine the milk, heavy cream, and sugar. Bring to a simmer over medium heat, whisking to dissolve the sugar, about 5 minutes. Remove the pan from the heat as soon as the mixture begins to simmer; do not boil. Add the bloomed gelatin and whisk until smooth and combined. Strain the mixture through a fine-mesh sieve into a medium bowl. Whisk in the almond extract.

3. Fill a large bowl with ice water. Place the medium bowl with the pudding mixture inside the ice bath. Whisk constantly until the pudding is slightly thickened and cold, about 5 minutes.

4. Pour the pudding into a deep serving dish and cover the dish with plastic wrap. Refrigerate until set, about 3 hours and up to overnight.

5. MAKE THE SYRUP: In a small saucepan, combine 1 cup water and the sugar. Bring to a boil over high heat and cook, stirring, until the sugar is dissolved, about 3 minutes. Pour the syrup into a heatproof bowl and let cool to room temperature. Add the amaretto (if using), cover, and refrigerate until cold, about 30 minutes. It will keep refrigerated for up to 2 weeks.

6. Use a spoon to scoop the pudding into four small bowls. Pour about ¼ cup of syrup into each bowl. Top with goji berries, if desired.

tip | Cooling the pudding over an ice bath instead of cooling at room temperature prevents the milk and heavy cream from separating into two layers.

Fruit Salad
with Rose Syrup

フルーツポンチ

This dessert is reminiscent of a fruit cocktail, but in Japanese, it's called "fruits ponchi." The focus is on the fruits, which are cut into bite-size pieces and soaked with a simple syrup. This is a very nostalgic dessert for me because it was served at my elementary school for lunch. I've added rose water for a floral note, which I love but you can omit if you don't like the flavor. It is another great dessert for making in advance and bringing to a potluck since it's easy to transport and looks beautiful. You can swap in any seasonal fruits, just make sure to not pick fruits that are too soft or delicate, such as raspberries or overripe bananas. The fruit salad can be eaten at room temperature or cold, in which case make sure to refrigerate for at least 30 minutes in step 2.

Serves 4 to 6

ROSE SYRUP

½ cup (100g) sugar

2 teaspoons rose water

FRUITS

1 mango, peeled and cut into 1-inch cubes

¼ melon, peeled, seeded, and cut into 1-inch pieces (about 1½ cups)

¼ pineapple, peeled, cored, and cut into 1-inch pieces (about 1 cup)

1 kiwi fruit, peeled and cut into 1-inch pieces

2 plums, pitted and cut into 1-inch wedges

1. MAKE THE ROSE SYRUP: In a saucepan, combine the sugar and 1½ cups water. Bring to a boil over medium-high heat and cook, stirring occasionally, until the sugar is completely dissolved, about 3 minutes. Remove the saucepan from the heat and add the rose water. Let cool to room temperature.

2. PREPARE THE FRUITS: In a 1-quart mason jar, large glass jar, large Tupperware, or large bowl, layer the mango, melon, pineapple, kiwi, and plums; you want to evenly distribute them. Pour in the cooled rose syrup and close the jar (or cover with plastic wrap). The fruit salad will keep in the refrigerator for up to 2 days. Serve the fruit salad at room temperature or chilled.

tips | You could make a refreshing drink out of this recipe. Add a small amount of the fruit salad to a glass and top with sparkling water.

• You could replace the rose water with orange blossom water.

Coffee Jelly

コーヒーゼリー

Coffee jelly is one of those desserts I never see in the US but is available just about everywhere in Japan. I remember my grandmother serving coffee jelly at her kissaten (Japanese tearoom and café). She presented it in a small glass bowl with Coffee mate. I like to pour half-and-half over mine and break it apart with a spoon, but you could also eat it with condensed milk or vanilla ice cream. Or try breaking it up and adding it to an iced coffee or latte for a bit of texture. At home, I make the jelly with drip coffee, but you're welcome to use your favorite method of brewing coffee—leftover morning coffee, cold brew, or even instant coffee will work well.

Serves 4

1 envelope (7g) unflavored gelatin powder

2 cups brewed coffee

2 tablespoons sugar

Half-and-half, for drizzling

1. Pour 1 tablespoon water into a small bowl. Sprinkle the gelatin over the water. Wait for 1 minute, then add another 1 tablespoon water to cover any dry spots. Set aside to bloom for 5 minutes.

2. In a small saucepan, combine the coffee and sugar. Cook over medium heat, whisking, until the sugar is dissolved, about 2 minutes. Remove the pan from the heat just before the coffee begins to simmer. Add the bloomed gelatin and stir to completely dissolve.

3. Pour into four small heatproof bowls or cups. Let cool to room temperature, then refrigerate until set, at least 3 hours. The jelly will keep refrigerated for up to 3 days.

4. Serve cold with half-and-half drizzled over the top.

Matcha and Black Sesame Cookies

抹茶と黒ごまのクッキー

This is one of my favorite butter cookies to serve in the afternoon with tea or coffee. You won't taste the flavor of almond flour, but it lends a beautiful crumbly texture. The sides of the cookies are crusted with a sesame sugar that provides a little crunch and nutty flavor. There are two kinds of matcha powders: the ceremonial grade for making tea and the culinary grade for baking. You can use culinary grade for these cookies, though if you want a more vivid green, I recommend trying ceremonial grade. I like to keep logs of the cookie dough in my freezer—they don't take up much space—and slice and bake whenever I have a sweet craving.

Makes 30 to 40 cookies

2 cups (260g) all-purpose flour

⅔ cup (65g) almond flour

1 tablespoon (6g) matcha powder

2 sticks (226g) unsalted butter, at room temperature

⅔ cup (135g) granulated sugar

1 large egg, at room temperature (see Tip, page 207), separated

2 tablespoons turbinado sugar

1 tablespoon toasted black sesame seeds

1. Using a fine-mesh sieve, sift the all-purpose flour, almond flour, and matcha powder into a medium bowl. If there are pieces of almond that remain in the sieve, add those to the bowl. Whisk to combine.

2. In a large bowl, using a handheld electric mixer, beat the butter and granulated sugar until pale and fluffy, about 3 minutes. Add the egg yolk and beat until well combined, about 1 minute. Add the flour mixture. Using a rubber spatula, stir until there are no visible flour streaks.

3. Divide the dough into two equal portions and place each one on a sheet of parchment paper. Roll each portion of dough into a 2-inch-diameter log, then wrap in the parchment. Wrap each parchment log with plastic and store in the refrigerator for at least 2 hours and up to 3 days. The cookie dough can be frozen for up to 3 months.

4. Preheat the oven to 325°F with racks in the upper and lower thirds. Line two baking sheets with parchment paper.

5. If you have a Japanese mortar and pestle, grind the turbinado sugar and sesame seeds in the mortar until coarsely ground. Alternatively, combine the turbinado sugar and black sesame seeds in a food processor or spice grinder. Pulse a few times until the sesame seeds are just starting to break down. Be careful not to overprocess.

6. Remove one cookie dough log from the refrigerator and remove the plastic and parchment. Brush the log with some egg white. Sprinkle the sesame-sugar mixture on a clean work surface or cutting board and roll the log in the mixture to evenly coat. Repeat with the second log.

(recipe continues)

7. Using a sharp knife, slice the logs crosswise into rounds ½ inch thick. Place the rounds on the prepared baking sheets, spacing them about 2 inches apart.

8. Bake, switching racks and rotating the sheets front to back halfway through, until the cookies are pale golden at the edges, 18 to 20 minutes. Keep an eye on the cookies as they are baking; you want the edges to just turn golden so that the matcha retains its vibrant green color.

9. Remove from the oven and let the cookies cool completely on the baking sheets. Cookies can be stored in an airtight container at room temperature for up to 5 days.

Strawberry and Sweet Bean Mochi

いちご大福

This seasonal confection is called ichigo daifuku in Japanese. It's a fresh strawberry that is wrapped in sweet bean paste and a thin layer of mochi. The juicy and tart strawberry marries beautifully with the sweet red beans and mochi. These treats are usually available in the late spring to early summer during peak strawberry season, when the berries are at their sweetest and juiciest. I love to eat them as an afternoon treat when I'm craving a sweet bite with a cup of tea.

Makes 10 pieces

1¼ cups (200g) sweet red bean paste, store-bought or homemade (page 227)

10 strawberries, stemmed

1 cup (150g) mochiko

⅓ cup (66g) sugar

Cornstarch or potato starch, for dusting

---

tips | You can use this mochi wrapper recipe to make mochi ice cream.

• The cooking time for the mochi will vary depending on your microwave wattage. My microwave is 1200W and it takes me about 6 minutes to make the mochi. If your wattage is lower, it might take longer.

1. Take 2 tablespoons of the red bean paste and roll it into a ball. Flatten the ball between the palms of your hands and wrap it around a strawberry. Make sure the pointy tip of the strawberry is just visible (it should poke out a bit), so you know where the stem end of the strawberry is. Repeat with the remaining red bean paste and strawberries. Refrigerate until ready to use.

2. In a microwave-safe medium bowl, whisk the mochiko and sugar. Add 1 cup water and whisk well until smooth (there should be no lumps). Cover the bowl with plastic wrap and microwave for 1 minute. Remove the plastic, being careful not to burn yourself with the steam. Using a wooden spatula or spoon, stir well. Repeat this process until the mochi dough is shiny and very stretchy,

almost like melted mozzarella, about 5 minutes total. After the 3-minute mark, the mochi will get sticky and gooey, dip the spatula in water before mixing the mochi to prevent it from sticking. Any tool that has direct contact with mochi (such as scissors, a knife, or a rolling pin) should be well dusted with cornstarch or potato starch. Use the mochi while it's warm. It'll become harder to handle as it cools down.

3. Dust a clean work surface or cutting board with ⅓ cup cornstarch. Divide the mochi dough into 10 portions. Working with one piece at a time, and using a rolling pin that's dusted with cornstarch, roll out the mochi into a disk that is twice as big as the sweet bean–covered strawberry (about 3½ inches in diameter).

(recipe continues)

4. Working with one at a time, wrap a covered strawberry in mochi. Twist the bottom (stem end of the strawberry) to close completely. Using scissors, cut away any excess dough, if necessary.

5. Place the strawberry and sweet bean mochi in paper cupcake liners or on a plate. To store, dust an airtight container with cornstarch before adding the mochi and then seal tightly. They will keep in the refrigerator for up to 2 days.

Sweet Red Bean Paste

あんこ

Anko is a sweet red bean paste that is used in many traditional Japanese confections. It's usually made with adzuki beans (small red beans) that are available at most health and natural foods stores or online. Unlike other beans, you don't need to soak these overnight. You can buy premade anko at Asian or Japanese grocery stores, but if you make it from scratch, you can control the sweetness. My recipe is less sweet than the store-bought version. You can use the anko for the Strawberry and Sweet Bean Mochi (page 223), as an ice cream topping, folded into whipped cream, or spread onto toast the way you would jam.

Makes about 2¼ cups

1 cup (200g) adzuki beans

¾ cup (150g) sugar

¼ teaspoon kosher salt

tips | Once you add the sugar, the adzuki beans will stop cooking, so make sure to first check that the beans are cooked through and tender. The older the beans are, the longer they'll take to cook.

• Unlike most homemade jams, anko won't last long in the refrigerator. My preferred way of storing the paste is to portion it out and freeze it.

1. Rinse the adzuki beans in a sieve and drain well. Transfer the beans to a medium pot or Dutch oven and add 3 cups water. Bring to a boil over high heat and cook until the water turns a deep burgundy color, 10 to 15 minutes. Drain the beans and wash the pot. (This step is called shibukiri in Japanese and removes any bitterness from the beans.)

2. Return the beans to the pot and add 3 cups water. Bring to a simmer over medium-low heat and cook, skimming frequently to remove any impurities that rise to the surface, until tender, about 30 minutes. The beans should always be covered with water as they cook; add more water as needed. Check if the beans are tender by tasting one or squishing it between your fingers.

3. Add about half of the sugar (6 tablespoons, or just eyeball it). Stir well with a silicone spatula. Add the remaining sugar and stir well. Simmer the beans, stirring occasionally, until most of the water has evaporated and the beans are mostly broken down, about 30 minutes. The mixture will look like a paste with some visible bean pieces. If you prefer a smoother paste, mash the beans with the back of a spatula or fork. Remove the pot from the heat and stir in the salt.

4. Spread the bean paste out on a sheet pan in an even layer. Cover with plastic wrap, with the plastic directly touching the beans. Let cool to room temperature. The paste will keep in an airtight container in the refrigerator for up to 3 days. To freeze the bean paste, divide it into small portions and wrap in plastic. Frozen paste will keep for up to 1 month.

Shokupan

食パン

Shokupan—which literally means "eating bread" but is often translated as milk bread—is a white sandwich bread. It's square and a little bigger and fluffier than American white bread. Its flavor is subtly sweet, and it has a tender crumb and a thin, soft crust. I love to use this bread for sandwiches or breakfast toast. In grocery stores in Japan, the loaves of bread are sliced more or less thick depending on the use: 5 to 6 slices (thick cut) for morning toast, and 8 slices for sandwiches. For Japanese-style toast, cut the bread 1 inch thick.

My mom would sometimes make pizza toast: Spread marinara sauce on a slice, then top with cheese and sliced onions and heat it up in a toaster oven. For a sweet option, I love spreading a piece of bread with butter, sprinkling with cinnamon sugar, topping with a sliced apple, and baking in the toaster oven. Or if you have leftover Sweet Red Bean Paste (page 227), try slathering it on a slice of buttered toast.

Makes 1 loaf

---

3 cups plus 2 tablespoons (375g) bread flour

½ teaspoon kosher salt

¾ cup (180g) warm water

⅓ cup (80g) warm whole milk

---

2 tablespoons honey

---

1 teaspoon (3g) active dry yeast

---

2 tablespoons plus 2 teaspoons (40g) unsalted butter, at room temperature

---

Neutral oil, such as canola or grapeseed, for greasing

---

1. In a large bowl, combine the bread flour and salt. Stir well.

2. In a medium bowl or glass measuring cup, combine the warm water, milk, honey, and yeast. Stir well.

3. Make a well in the center of the flour mixture and pour in the milk mixture. Using your hands or a bowl scraper, mix well until the dough comes together. Turn the dough out onto a lightly floured work surface and knead until smooth and shiny, about 10 minutes. (Alternatively, use a stand mixer with the dough hook and mix on medium speed until the dough is smooth and shiny, about 5 minutes.)

4. Flatten the dough and wrap the butter in the dough. Knead until the butter is well incorporated and the dough is no longer greasy, about 10 minutes. (If using a stand mixer, use a rubber spatula to slightly flatten

out the dough in the bowl. Add the butter and fold the dough over the butter to enclose. Using the dough hook, mix on medium speed until the butter is incorporated, 5 to 7 minutes.)

5. Shape the dough into a ball, tucking the edges under the bottom. Pinch to close the seam. Lightly grease a medium bowl with oil. Place the dough in the bowl, seam-side down. Cover with plastic wrap or a damp towel. Let rise at room temperature until doubled in size, about 1 hour.

6. Transfer the proofed dough to a lightly floured work surface. Punch the dough a few times to release the gas. Weigh the dough on a scale and divide it into two equal portions. Shape each piece into a ball and cover them with plastic wrap or a damp towel. Let rest for 15 minutes.

7. Grease an 8 × 5 × 4½-inch Pullman loaf pan with oil. Make sure the pan has a lid. Set aside.

8. Roll one ball of dough into an oval shape about 12 inches long and 6 inches wide. Fold the long sides of the dough in to meet in the center. Starting with the short side, roll the dough into a log. Pinch to close the seam. Repeat with the other ball of dough.

9. Place the dough logs side by side in the pan, seam-side down, with a sliver of space between the logs. Cover with plastic wrap and let rise in a warm, draft-free place until the dough is 1 inch below the rim of the pan, about 45 minutes. (The ideal ambient temperature for the second proofing is 95°F.)

10. Preheat the oven to 425°F.

11. Cover the pan with the lid and transfer to the oven. Reduce the oven temperature to 400°F and bake, rotating the pan front to back halfway through, until golden brown, about 40 minutes.

12. Remove the pan from the oven and carefully drop the pan on a flat surface once or twice to help release excess air from the bread. (This prevents the bread from shrinking too much.) Remove the lid and unmold the bread onto a wire rack. Let cool completely, about 2 hours. The bread is best eaten on the first or second day. It can be refrigerated up to 3 days. Alternatively, slices can be wrapped in plastic and frozen for up to 1 month.

(recipe continues)

tips | The desired temperature for the milk-water mixture is around 98°F. I usually microwave it for 10 seconds, stir well, and dip my finger in to check the temperature. It should be almost the same temperature as your skin.

• When you proof the dough, you can leave it in a warm spot in the kitchen, but make sure it's not too hot as this can cause overproofing. If the dough is overproofed, the yeast eats up the sugar and the bread won't have much flavor.

• If you have leftover slices that are going stale, use them to make French toast.

Melon Pan

メロンパン

Melon pan is a crunchy sweet bun similar to a Mexican concha. Despite its name, it's not flavored with melon. There are a few stories behind its name—one says that the grid pattern on the top resembles that on the skin of a melon. I especially love the contrast of textures: a crackly cookie shell on the outside, and the soft pillowy texture of the crumb inside. I'll usually eat melon pan for breakfast with a cup of milky coffee. When I was in high school and my mom didn't have time to make a bento, she would give me an allowance of five dollars. Of course, I would use the money to buy only sweet breads and buns for lunch, and this is one I'd always get.

Makes 8 buns

COOKIE DOUGH

2 tablespoons (28g) unsalted butter, at room temperature

2 tablespoons granulated sugar

1 large egg, at room temperature, whisked

⅔ cup (86g) all-purpose flour

¼ cup (30g) almond flour

BUNS

½ cup (120g) whole milk

1 tablespoon granulated sugar

1 teaspoon (3g) active dry yeast

2 cups (260g) all-purpose flour

1 large egg, whisked

½ teaspoon kosher salt

1 tablespoon (14g) unsalted butter, at room temperature, cut into small pieces

2 tablespoons turbinado or granulated sugar

tips | When you make the topping, if the egg is too cold, the butter and egg mixture might break. If the mixture looks broken, add 1 tablespoon almond flour from the ¼ cup and whisk until smooth.

• If you keep the bread for more than 2 days, you will want to warm it up in the oven for a few minutes.

1. MAKE THE COOKIE DOUGH: Place the butter in a medium bowl. Using a whisk or a handheld electric mixer, beat the butter on high speed until pale and fluffy. Add the granulated sugar and beat to incorporate. Add the egg in two additions, beating each time to combine. Sift in the all-purpose and almond flours. Using a rubber spatula, mix until well combined.

2. Transfer the cookie dough to a piece of plastic wrap and press into a flat rectangle. Wrap in plastic and refrigerate for 30 minutes.

3. Divide the dough into 8 equal portions and roll each one into a ball (they should be about 28g each). Refrigerate until ready to use.

4. MAKE THE BUNS: Pour the milk into a microwave-safe bowl or liquid measuring cup. Microwave in 10-second intervals until the milk reaches 110° to 115°F, about 30 seconds. (Alternatively, heat the milk in a small saucepan over medium-low heat.) Dip your finger into the milk; it should feel a little hotter than a hot shower. Add ½ tablespoon of the granulated sugar and the yeast to the milk. Whisk to combine and set aside until very foamy, about 10 minutes.

(recipe continues)

5. In a large bowl, combine the flour, egg, and remaining ½ tablespoon granulated sugar. Pour the yeast mixture over the flour mixture. Using a rubber or wooden spatula, mix until a dough comes together.

6. Transfer the dough to a clean work surface. Add the salt and knead until the dough is elastic, about 5 minutes. Add the butter and knead until the butter is incorporated. At first, the dough may look separated, but keep kneading until it comes together and is very smooth and shiny. Shape the dough into a ball and place it in a large bowl. Cover with plastic wrap and let rest in a warm place until doubled in size, about 1 hour.

7. Remove the plastic and gently punch the dough to release the gas. Divide the dough into 8 equal pieces. Shape each piece into a 2-inch ball by gently stretching the dough and pinching at the bottom. Make a very smooth and round surface. Cover the buns with plastic wrap or a damp towel. Let rest for 10 minutes.

8. Cut two 5-inch square pieces of parchment paper. Place a cookie dough ball between the parchment squares and roll it out into a 3-inch-diameter disk. It should be slightly bigger than the buns. Peel off the top piece of parchment paper. Flip the cookie dough disk over onto a bun, gently press the cookie dough against the bun, and peel off the other piece of parchment paper. Repeat with the remaining cookie dough balls and buns.

9. Place the turbinado sugar in a small bowl. Dip the cookie dough side of the buns into the sugar to evenly coat. Using a sharp knife, score the cookie dough in a grid pattern.

10. Line two baking sheets with parchment paper. Transfer the buns to the prepared sheets, spacing them 2 inches apart. Cover with plastic wrap or a kitchen towel. Let rest until doubled in size, 45 minutes to 1 hour.

11. Preheat the oven to 350°F with the racks in the upper and lower thirds.

12. Bake, switching racks and rotating the sheets front to back halfway through, until the buns are slightly golden, about 15 minutes.

13. Transfer the buns to a wire rack and let cool to room temperature. The buns will keep in an airtight container at room temperature for up to 3 days, or tightly wrapped in plastic and frozen for up to 1 month.

Citrus Mochi Doughnuts

シトラス風味のもちドーナツ

This is my ode to Mister Donut, Japan's most popular doughnut chain. Their doughnuts are chewy and fluffy and bouncy—a texture unlike anything I've found at other doughnut shops. I ate so many of these when I was living in Japan. The secret ingredient is tofu, but you won't taste it. The tofu hydrates the dough and gives it a nice firm texture. I've chosen to re-create the "Pon de Ring" doughnut, which is shaped like a flower. Mine are dipped in a citrus glaze and sprinkled with a lime-lemon sugar for a double dose of citrus. The zesty sugar looks beautiful, too. As a bonus, this is one of the easiest doughnut recipes, with a very impressive final result. You can have the doughnuts formed and fried in an hour.

Makes 4 doughnuts

DOUGHNUTS

7 ounces medium-firm tofu, drained and patted dry

½ cup shiratamako (60g) or mochiko (75g)

1 tablespoon fresh lemon juice

½ cup (65g) all-purpose flour

¼ cup (50g) granulated sugar

1 tablespoon potato starch or cornstarch

2 teaspoons baking powder

Pinch of kosher salt

Neutral oil, such as canola or grapeseed, for frying

CITRUS SUGAR AND GLAZE

1 tablespoon granulated sugar

1 teaspoon grated lemon zest

1 teaspoon grated lime zest

1 cup (120g) powdered sugar

1 tablespoon fresh lemon juice

1 tablespoon fresh lime juice

tips | The doughnuts are best eaten fresh. They lose their crisp exterior overnight.

• You can also coat the doughnuts with cinnamon sugar or melted chocolate.

1. MAKE THE DOUGHNUTS: Cut four 4-inch squares of parchment paper.

2. In a medium bowl, combine the tofu, shiratamako, and lemon juice. Use your hands to combine the ingredients, crumbling the tofu and mixing well. The mixture should look like cottage cheese. Add the all-purpose flour, granulated sugar, potato starch, baking powder, and salt. Mix well with your hands until the dough comes together and is firm. When you press the dough with a finger, the imprint should remain.

3. Divide the dough into 24 equal portions, about 1 tablespoon each. Roll each portion into a ball. Working on one square of parchment paper, connect 6 balls to form a ring, making sure the balls stick to each other. Repeat with the remaining balls and parchment paper squares to make a total of 4 doughnut rings. (At this point, the doughnuts can be individually wrapped in plastic and refrigerated overnight or frozen for up to 1 month; if frozen, thaw in the refrigerator overnight before frying.)

(recipe continues)

4. Pour about 2 inches of oil into a large deep pot or Dutch oven. Heat the oil over medium heat until it registers 320°F on a deep-fry thermometer. Place one square of parchment paper with the doughnut ring on a large slotted spoon or spatula and gently lower it into the oil. Repeat with a second doughnut. Fry the two doughnuts until golden and crispy, 3 to 4 minutes. The parchment paper will separate from the doughnut; remove the paper with tongs or a spoon and discard. Transfer the doughnuts to a wire rack. Repeat with the remaining doughnuts. Let cool to room temperature.

5. MAKE THE CITRUS SUGAR AND GLAZE: In a small bowl, combine the granulated sugar, lemon zest, and lime zest. Mix the citrus sugar well.

6. In a medium bowl, combine the powdered sugar, lemon juice, and lime juice. Mix the citrus glaze until smooth.

7. Working one at a time, dip one side of a doughnut into the glaze. Transfer to a wire rack and sprinkle with the citrus sugar. Let the glaze harden, about 5 minutes.

Pork Buns

肉まん

In Japan, convenience stores start selling steamed buns when it gets cold. There are many types of fillings, including my childhood favorite, marinara sauce and cheese (called "pizzaman" in Japanese). I've chosen a classic bun with pork called nikuman. For a sweet version, replace the pork filling with Sweet Red Bean Paste (page 227), use grapeseed oil instead of sesame oil in the dough, and follow the same cooking directions below.

Makes 8 buns

DOUGH

2 cups (260g) all-purpose flour, plus more for dusting

1 tablespoon sugar

1 teaspoon (3g) instant (rapid-rise) yeast

A pinch of kosher salt

½ cup plus 1 tablespoon room-temperature water

1 tablespoon toasted sesame oil

FILLING

½ pound ground pork

2 scallions, finely chopped

1 teaspoon finely grated fresh ginger

1 tablespoon sake

1 teaspoon soy sauce

2 teaspoons toasted sesame oil

½ teaspoon kosher salt

1. Cut eight 2-inch square pieces of parchment paper. Set aside.

2. MAKE THE DOUGH: In a large bowl, combine the flour, sugar, yeast, and salt. Using chopsticks or a whisk, mix together. Add the water and mix until a shaggy dough forms. Mix in the sesame oil. Turn the dough out onto a lightly floured work surface and knead until smooth, about 5 minutes. If the dough is tough, wet your hands and knead until the dough absorbs the water. Rest the dough for 5 minutes, then knead again until smooth, about 3 minutes.

3. Shape the dough into a ball and place in a bowl. Cover with plastic wrap or a damp towel and set aside at room temperature until the dough doubles in size, about 30 minutes. (Alternatively, refrigerate the dough overnight.)

4. MAKE THE FILLING: In a medium bowl, combine the pork, scallions, ginger, sake, soy sauce, sesame oil, and salt. Using your hands, mix until well combined. Set aside.

5. Place the dough on a lightly floured work surface and shape it into a log. Divide the dough into 8 equal portions. Roll each portion into a ball. Using a rolling pin, roll the dough into a thin disk, about 4 inches in diameter and ⅛ inch thick.

6. Working with one at a time, place about 1 tablespoon filling in the center of each disk. Pull opposite sides of the dough toward the middle and pinch them together, pinching and twisting the dough at the top to close the bun and ensure that the filling stays inside. If the filling escapes from the dough, use the back ends of chopsticks or a small spoon to push the filling back into the dough. Place each bun on a square of parchment paper. Place the pork buns in a steamer basket, spacing them 1 inch apart. (If you don't have a steamer, see Tip, page 211.)

7. Add 1 inch of water to a large pot and bring to a boil over high heat. Wrap the underside of the lid with a kitchen towel to prevent condensation from dripping onto the buns. Make sure to tie the ends of the towel over the top of the lid so the fabric doesn't catch on fire.

8. Once the water comes to a boil, reduce the heat to medium and bring to a simmer. Place the steamer basket inside the pot and cover with the towel-wrapped lid. Cook until the filling is cooked through, about 15 minutes. (Check if the filling is cooked through by inserting a cake tester or chopstick into a bun; the juices should run clear.) Using tongs, carefully transfer the buns to a serving plate.

9. Serve immediately or wait a few minutes for the buns to cool. (Careful, they can be very hot!) The buns will keep in an airtight container in the refrigerator for up to 2 days, or individually wrapped in plastic and frozen for up to 1 month.

how to sando

Sandwiches, known as sandos in Japanese, are as popular as onigiri (rice balls) and can be found just about everywhere: supermarkets, convenience stores, train stations. . . . They are always made with soft slices of shokupan (milk bread) and filled with a variety of ingredients. The sandwiches are usually cut into triangles and neatly wrapped in plastic. I've included my three favorite fillings here.

You can make shokupan from scratch (page 228) or buy it at an Asian bakery. In a pinch, you can substitute with a soft white sandwich bread. Shokupan has a slightly sweeter crumb and the slices are bigger than most American sandwich breads, so you may have to adjust the amount of filling.

Strawberry and Cream Sandos いちごサンド

Fruit sandos—pieces of fresh fruit and whipped cream sandwiched between soft slices of shokupan—are a very popular dessert in Japan. You can swap in and combine any fresh fruit you like, such as kiwi, banana, mango, and figs, though avoid watery fruits, such as watermelon, as they'll dilute the cream. Since this sandwich is quite rich, I recommend two small triangles per person. You could easily double or triple the recipe to make a larger quantity. These sandos are easy to transport; just keep them wrapped in plastic and slice right before serving.

Makes 8 small sandwiches (serves 4)

½ cup mascarpone

½ cup heavy cream

2 tablespoons powdered sugar

4 (½-inch-thick) slices Shokupan (page 228) or store-bought milk bread

½ teaspoon vanilla extract

10 to 12 strawberries, washed, dried, and stemmed

1. In a medium bowl, combine the mascarpone, heavy cream, and powdered sugar. Using a whisk or a handheld electric mixer, whisk until stiff peaks form.

2. Place the slices of shokupan on a cutting board or clean work surface. Spread about 2 tablespoons of the whipped cream mixture onto each slice of bread. Place 5 strawberries, on their sides, onto 2 slices of bread, forming an X. You can add more strawberries if there's space. Top with the other 2 slices of bread, cream-side down.

3. Wrap each sandwich with plastic and refrigerate for 10 minutes and up to 2 hours.

4. Unwrap the sandwiches. Using a serrated knife, cut away and discard the crusts. Cut each sandwich on a diagonal into quarters to make 4 triangles. You want to cut along the strawberries to halve them. (You are following the X shape.) Serve immediately.

tips | Though you want the cream to be firm enough to spread, be careful not to overwhip the cream, or it'll start to turn grainy.

• I add mascarpone to the heavy cream to give the whipped cream more body and thickness. You can use all heavy cream if you prefer, in which case omit the mascarpone and use 1 cup heavy cream.

• You can replace the vanilla extract with 1 teaspoon brandy or rum for a spiked sando.

• If you want to make these ahead, prep all the ingredients beforehand and assemble the sandwiches a few hours before serving. If you assemble the sandwiches too far in advance, the fruit will release moisture and the bread can get soggy. The cream can be whipped up to 3 hours in advance; just refrigerate and whisk it a few times if it becomes loose.

(recipe continues)

Egg Salad Sandos たまごサンド

My mom usually made my bento with onigiri, but every now and again, she would put in a tamago (egg) sando and a ham and cucumber sando. It was always such a nice surprise. This recipe calls for separating the egg yolks from the whites. It's an extra step, but this way you can make creamy and fluffy convenience store–style egg sandwiches.

Makes 16 small sandwiches (serves 4)

6 large eggs

8 (½-inch-thick) slices Shokupan (page 228) or store-bought milk bread

¼ cup plus 8 teaspoons mayonnaise, preferably Kewpie

½ teaspoon sugar

Kosher salt and freshly ground black pepper

1. Place the eggs in a small pot. Cover with water. Turn the heat to medium and set a timer for 13 minutes. Bring to a boil, then reduce the heat to medium and simmer until the timer goes off. Meanwhile, fill a large bowl with ice water. Drain the eggs and transfer to the bowl of ice water. Set aside until cool enough to touch.

2. Peel the eggs and pat dry if they are wet. Cut in half and separate the yolks from the whites. Place the egg yolks in a bowl and the egg whites on a cutting board.

3. Add ¼ cup of the mayonnaise and the sugar to the yolks. Using a rubber spatula or a fork, mash the yolks until very smooth, whipping to add some air. They should be quite fluffy. Season with salt and pepper.

4. Finely chop the egg whites and add them to the egg yolk mixture. Mix well to combine.

5. Place the shokupan slices on a cutting board or clean work surface. Spread one side of each slice with 1 teaspoon mayonnaise. Evenly divide the egg salad among 4 slices of bread (about ½ cup per bread). Top with the other 4 slices of bread, mayonnaise-side down. Wrap the sandwiches in plastic, then stack them one on top of the other. Refrigerate for 10 minutes.

6. Unwrap the sandwiches. Using a serrated knife, cut away and discard the crusts. Cut each sandwich on the diagonal into quarters. Serve immediately.

tips | When I'm cooking many hard-boiled eggs at a time, I like to add the eggs to the water and then turn on the heat. This way the eggs are less likely to break and you don't need a slotted spoon. But use your trusted method if you already have one.

• By stacking the sandwiches, their weight naturally presses down and allows the filling to better stick to the bread.

• The egg salad can be refrigerated for up to 1 day and the sandwiches assembled up to 2 hours before serving, though they're best assembled right before eating.

Katsu Sandos カツサンド

Katsu sando—pork cutlet sandwich—is a great way to use leftover tonkatsu. Sometimes I'll make a double batch of pork cutlets so I have extra for sandos, or if I have just a few leftover cutlets, I'll make myself one or two sandos for lunch the next day. (You can halve the recipe below to make two sandwiches.) I almost always make a cabbage salad (see Cabbage Salad with Lemon-Miso Dressing, page 54) to serve alongside the tonkatsu, so I purposely save a bit of thinly sliced cabbage for making a sando the next day. Even though you're using the same ingredients, they transform into something completely different. If you can't find a store-bought tonkatsu sauce, you can substitute with an equal amount of barbecue sauce or 2 teaspoons Worcestershire sauce.

Makes 8 small sandwiches (serves 4)

¼ cup plus 2 tablespoons store-bought tonkatsu sauce, such as Bull-Dog brand

2 tablespoons ketchup

8 (½-inch-thick) slices Shokupan (page 228) or store-bought milk bread

8 teaspoons Dijon mustard or yellow mustard

1 cup thinly sliced green cabbage

8 fried pork cutlets (Tonkatsu, page 87)

1. In a small bowl, combine the tonkatsu sauce and ketchup. Set aside.

2. Place the slices of shokupan on a cutting board or clean work surface. Spread 1 teaspoon of mustard on one side of each slice. Top 4 slices of the shokupan with ¼ cup of cabbage each.

3. Place 2 pork cutlets on a plate. Using the back of a spoon, spread 1 tablespoon of the tonkatsu-ketchup mixture on top of both pork cutlets. Place the pork cutlets, side by side and sauce-side down, over the cabbage on a bread slice. Drizzle 1 tablespoon of the tonkatsu-ketchup mixture over the cutlets. Top with a slice of bread, mustard-side down. Repeat with the remaining ingredients.

4. Wrap each sandwich in plastic wrap. Stack the sandwiches and place a weight, such as a small plate, on top of the sandwiches to press them. Set aside for 5 minutes.

5. Unwrap the sandwiches. Using a serrated knife, cut away and discard the crusts. Cut each sandwich on the diagonal into halves and serve.

epilogue

In early 2021, my mother was diagnosed with stage 4 cancer. She passed away in the middle of my writing this cookbook. Not a day goes by that I don't think about her and wish she were here to celebrate the book's publication.

Until the very end, I would ask her questions about my favorite childhood recipes, many of which I've included in the book. She would give me instructions, but never with precise measurements; it was always a handful of this, a splash of that. Everything was eyeballed. Even when she sent me a video of how to make kakiage (fritters), I had to guess the amounts just by rewatching her gestures. Instead of using measurements, she thought in ratios: one part this, two parts that. Maybe because we were a family of five and left home one by one until it was just my mom and dad—she often had to adjust her recipes based on how many mouths she was feeding.

My mom was the youngest of three, and the only daughter. Her brothers moved to other prefectures, whereas she stayed in Hiroshima, close to her parents. She helped her mom run a kissaten (Japanese tearoom and café). At age twenty-three, she married my dad and was pregnant with me the following year. We had very few restaurants or take-out spots nearby, so she prepared almost every meal from scratch. The last time I was in Japan, she was tired and frail, but insisted on cooking for me. Each time I offered to help, she would gently scold me, telling me to sit down and relax. Cooking was her way of showing love: waking up early to prepare a breakfast of many dishes, filling our house with the buttery scent of madeleines, shaping onigiri (rice balls) with piping-hot rice for lunch. The skin on her hands was a bit rough from years of cooking and washing dishes—hardworking hands that nourished us every day.

Lately, I've been thinking about how I'll never be like my mother. She was athletic, adventurous, and had countless hobbies, such as calligraphy and playing both the shamisen and koto (traditional

Japanese string instruments). In her fifties, she persuaded my dad to go skydiving with her in Bali. She had high standards for herself and was never satisfied. And yet everything she did in the kitchen looked effortless and easy, whether she was assembling a simple lunch or baking cream puffs. Her food was prepared and presented in the most beautiful manner. Since I was more interested in food than my siblings, it was something special that we shared. I would learn about new food trends through her. You could say she was my food influencer.

Most of all, my mom embodied her name, Yoko (陽子), which in Japanese means "sun child." She was incredibly charming and had a wonderful sense of humor. Unlike my dad, who has a more serious demeanor, she was always joking. True to her name, she radiated palpable warmth, and the few times she was sick or absent from the kitchen, it felt as though the sun had disappeared. Even with the lights turned on, the kitchen would be dim and cold.

When I returned to Japan for her funeral, I cooked for my family. It was strange and disorienting to be in the kitchen without her. I made Japanese breakfast: grilled fish, tamagoyaki (rolled omelet), and miso soup. I used a dried fish she had portioned out and frozen beforehand. As I cooked and moved around the kitchen, I noticed how impeccably positioned everything was. At first glance, the kitchen didn't seem particularly tidy from all the clutter and stacks of ceramic plates, but it became apparent that the ingredients, cooking tools, and tableware were positioned exactly in the right place, at arm's reach. She had a system that made perfect sense, a testament to how efficient and organized she was.

When I told my mom I was writing a cookbook, she was excited and happy for me, but I don't know how seriously she took it. Aside from saying "Sugoi!" ("Wow, how cool!"), she didn't ask much about it, maybe because most Japanese cookbooks are thin and look like magazines. Whereas for me, writing a cookbook is the greatest accomplishment. At the same time, since we loved to talk about food, the book was at the center of our exchanges. I told her about the recipes I wanted to include, I asked dozens of questions about amounts and measurements (to varying degrees of success), and I took photos of her dishes for reference. Often, I developed recipes from memory, trying to re-create the flavors and scents of the food I ate at home.

I worried that my mom didn't have a full life outside of being a parent, in part because I only saw her "mother" side. But after she died, many of her friends came to visit and pay their respects, some of them traveling long distances to our town. It was moving to see all the lives she had touched beyond our family unit, and how greatly loved she was. My mom never met my son, Hugo, who was born early in the pandemic. Whenever there's a milestone or something sweet happens, like Hugo holding his best friend's hand, I feel immense joy and sadness. I miss her so much and wish I could share those moments with her, especially all the ways her grandson is like her—his boundless energy, his silliness, how he fills a room with light. And, of course, to show her the finished book, not just to prove that it's heavier than a magazine, but so she can see how deeply she's shaped my life and the food I cook today. I feel fortunate that I finally have a place to record her recipes. I hope that by cooking from this book, you can also experience some of her warmth and brightness in your kitchen.

acknowledgments

Writing this cookbook made me realize that so many people are involved in making a book, and I cannot thank them enough. As I write these acknowledgments, I'm crying my eyes out, but here it goes.

Sanaë Lemoine—I would be completely lost without you as my co-author. You made my first book-writing experience so much more pleasant and less lonely. I almost didn't want to finish writing the cookbook, so we could continue chatting weekly. Thank you for everything. I cherish the friendship we've built through writing this book.

Susan Vu—you are my biggest cheerleader! This book wouldn't exist without your encouragement. Thank you for testing most of the recipes, including baking bread and roasting a whole chicken in the middle of an LA summer. I'm so honored to call you my friend.

Jun Tan—I'm forever grateful for having you as my mentor. Thank you for being my teacher, sharing your knowledge, and answering my endless questions about baking.

Hitomi Aihara and Jihee Kim, for testing recipes, helping me during the photo shoot, and being awesome friends!

My editor, Jennifer Sit, who reached out to me. My heart stopped for a second when I saw your email in my inbox. Thank you for giving me this opportunity and introducing me to incredible collaborators. And thank you to everyone else at Clarkson Potter who brought this book to life, including Bianca Cruz, Ashley Meyer, Claudia Wu, Mia Johnson, Christine Tanigawa, Kim Tyner, and Merri Ann Morrell.

My agent, Anthony Mattero, for believing in me and taking me under your wing.

My photographer, Jeni Afuso—I've been a huge fan of your work, and having you photograph this book was a dream come true. Thank you for capturing my recipes so beautifully.

The rest of the incredibly talented photo team—Kate Parisian, for going above and beyond for this project. Caroline Hwang, for making everything look delicious and so pretty. Thank you also to Jessica Darakjian and Joscha Krämer, and to Prop Link for letting me use your space and gorgeous props!

My dear friends who helped me navigate tough times and gave me endless support while making this book: Reiko Takekawa, Brando Bohorquez, Annie Jeong, Niki Ang, Sean Miura,

Akane McKirdy, Susan Kim, Jessica Massa, Hector Gomez, and Alvin Zhou.

My talented chef friends, for answering all cooking-related questions and sharing your wisdom: Luke Davin, Yuji Haraguchi, Gahee Kim, Gemma Matsuyama Yamada, Jimmy Sugi, and Ai Fujimoto of Omiso. Thank you, Cindy Tran, for testing my recipes along with Su.

Miyake Ceramics, for sending me lots of beautiful tableware from Japan. Ozma of California, for letting me wear your gorgeous outfits. Hasami Porcelain, Kinto, and Le Creuset for the lovely tableware, drinkware, and cookware.

My co-workers, past and present, from Tasty and BuzzFeed: It has been a privilege to work with such talented and hardworking people. I learn a lot from each one of you.

My viewers and followers on social media: Thank you so much for all the sweet comments and constant encouragement. You have no idea how much I appreciate all of you. When I test my recipes, I always think of you and how I can make my recipes easy and accessible. I hope you'll enjoy cooking from this book and sharing meals with your loved ones.

Finally, my deepest thanks to my family.

My family in Japan: My father and brother, and especially my sister, Yukiko, who can cook faster and more efficiently than I ever could. Thank you for teaching me Japanese cooking trends and hacks. You are the best.

My Texas family, especially my in-laws, Patricia and Brooke: Thank you for making me feel like a member of your family from day one.

Hugo, my love: You are very selective about what you like to eat, but I dream of the day when you'll eat everything from this book, and we can finally cook together.

Blair, the best partner I could ask for. Thank you for always giving me the most wonderful advice and supporting my dreams. I love you.

Mom, thank you for everything. I wish you were here.

お母さん、ありがとう。

index

Copyright © 2023 by Rie McClenny
Photographs copyright © 2023 by Jeni Afuso

All rights reserved.
Published in the United States by Clarkson Potter/Publishers, an imprint of the
Crown Publishing Group, a division of Penguin Random House LLC, New York.
ClarksonPotter.com

CLARKSON POTTER is a trademark and POTTER with colophon is a
registered trademark of Penguin Random House LLC.

Library of Congress Cataloging-in-Publication Data
Names: McClenny, Rie, author. | Lemoine, Sanaë, author. | Afuso, Jeni,
    photographer.
Title: Make it Japanese / Rie McClenny, with Sanaë Lemoine ; photographs
    by Jeni Afuso.
Description: New York : Clarkson Potter/Publishers, 2023 | Includes index.
Identifiers: LCCN 2022057813 (print) | LCCN 2022057814 (ebook) |
    ISBN 9780593236352 (hardcover) | ISBN 9780593236369 (ebook)
Subjects: LCSH: Cooking, Japanese. | LCGFT: Cookbooks.
Classification: LCC TX724.5.J3 M375 2023 (print) | LCC TX724.5.J3
    (ebook) | DDC 641.5952--dc23/eng/20221202
LC record available at https://lccn.loc.gov/2022057813
LC ebook record available at https://lccn.loc.gov/2022057814

ISBN 978-0-593-23635-2
Ebook ISBN 978-0-593-23636-9

Printed in China

Editor: Jennifer Sit
Editorial assistant: Bianca Cruz
Designer: Claudia Wu
Art director: Mia Johnson
Production editor: Christine Tanigawa
Production manager: Kim Tyner
Compositors: Merri Ann Morrell and Hannah Hunt
Food stylist: Caroline Hwang
Food stylist assistant: Jessica Darakjian
Prop stylist: Kate Parisian
Photo assistant: Joscha D. Krämer
Copyeditor: Kate Slate
Proofreader: Eldes Tran
Indexer: Elizabeth Parson
Publicist: Kristin Casemore
Marketer: Andrea Portanova

10 9 8 7 6 5 4 3 2 1

First Edition